MICHAEL JAC
Greatest H

Content

Published by

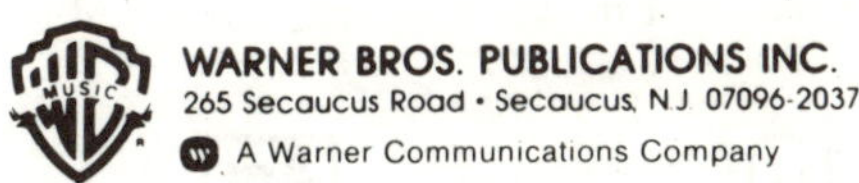

Exclusive Distributor

P.O. Box 27, New Berlin, WI 53151

Printed in U.S.A.

BAD

GUITAR
BIG 'N' BOLD
Medium ROCK

Words and Music by
MICHAEL JACKSON

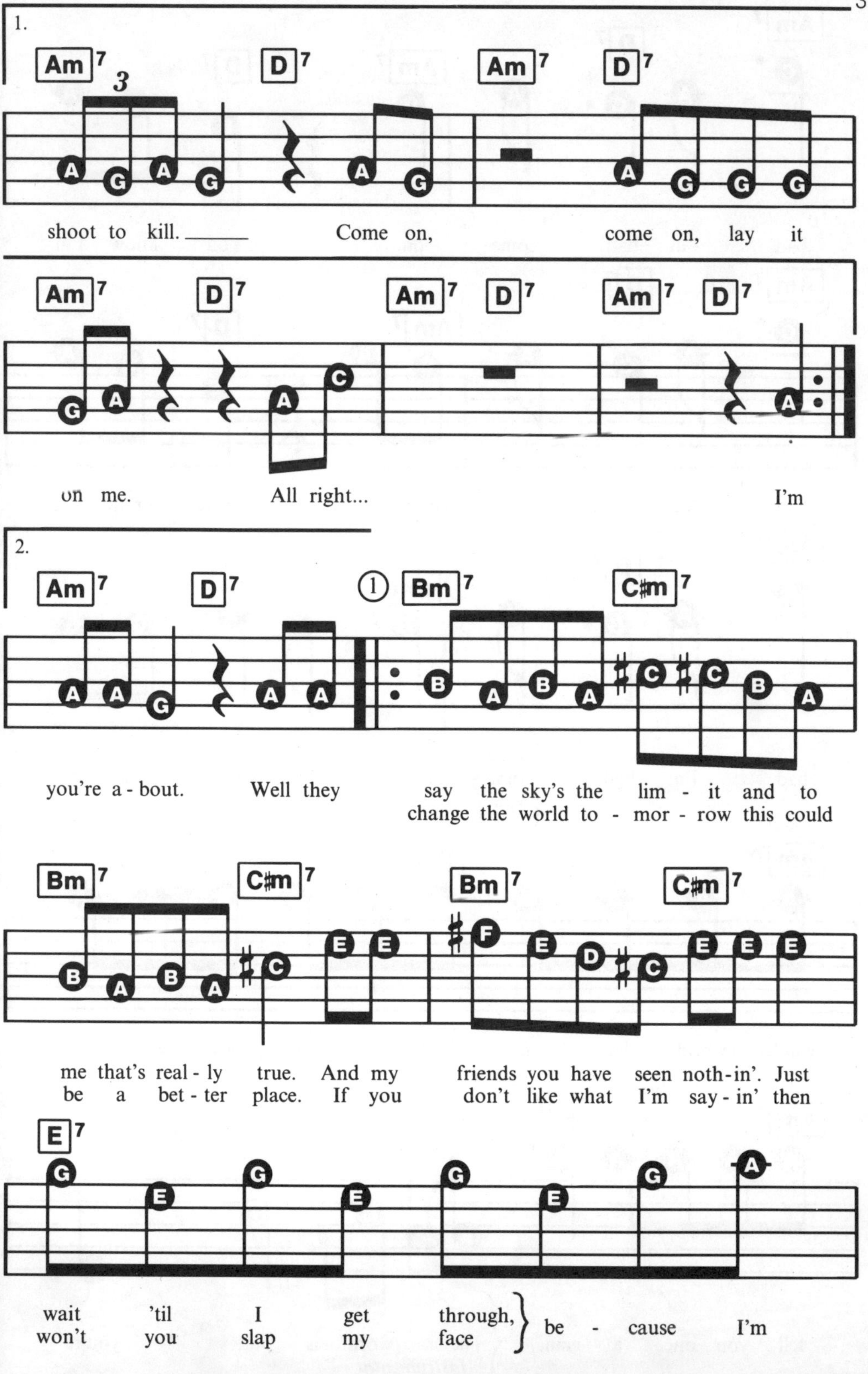

1.

Am7 D7 Am7 D7

shoot to kill. ______ Come on, come on, lay it

Am7 D7 Am7 D7 Am7 D7

on me. All right... I'm

2.

Am7 D7 ① Bm7 C#m7

you're a - bout. Well they say the sky's the lim - it and to
change the world to - mor - row this could

Bm7 C#m7 Bm7 C#m7

me that's real - ly true. And my friends you have seen noth - in'. Just
be a bet - ter place. If you don't like what I'm say - in' then

E7

wait 'til I get through,
won't you slap my face } be - cause I'm

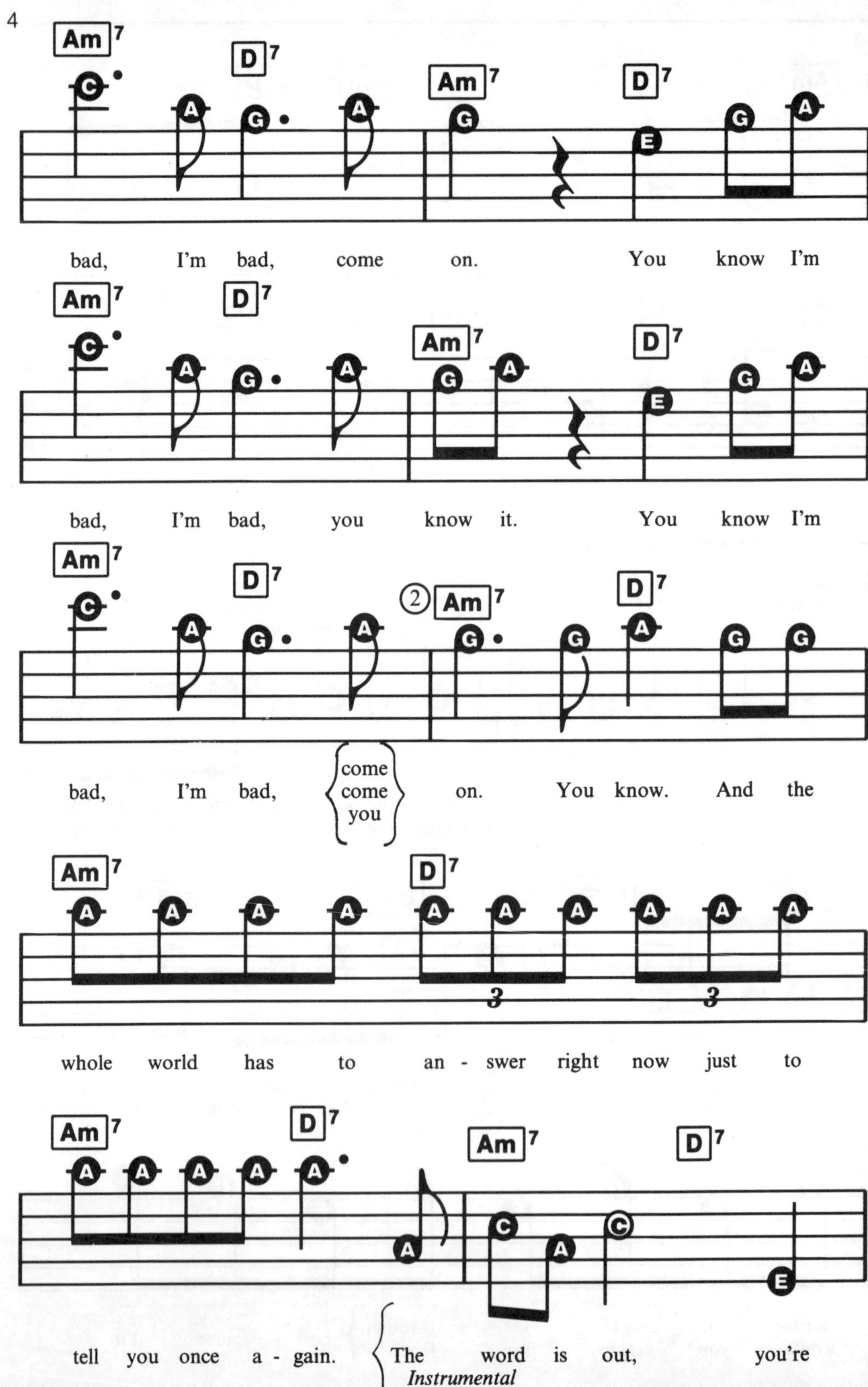
Am7
D7
bad, I'm bad, come on. You know I'm
bad, I'm bad, you know it. You know I'm
bad, I'm bad, come come you on. You know. And the
2
whole world has to an - swer right now just to
3
3
tell you once a - gain. The word is out, you're
Instrumental

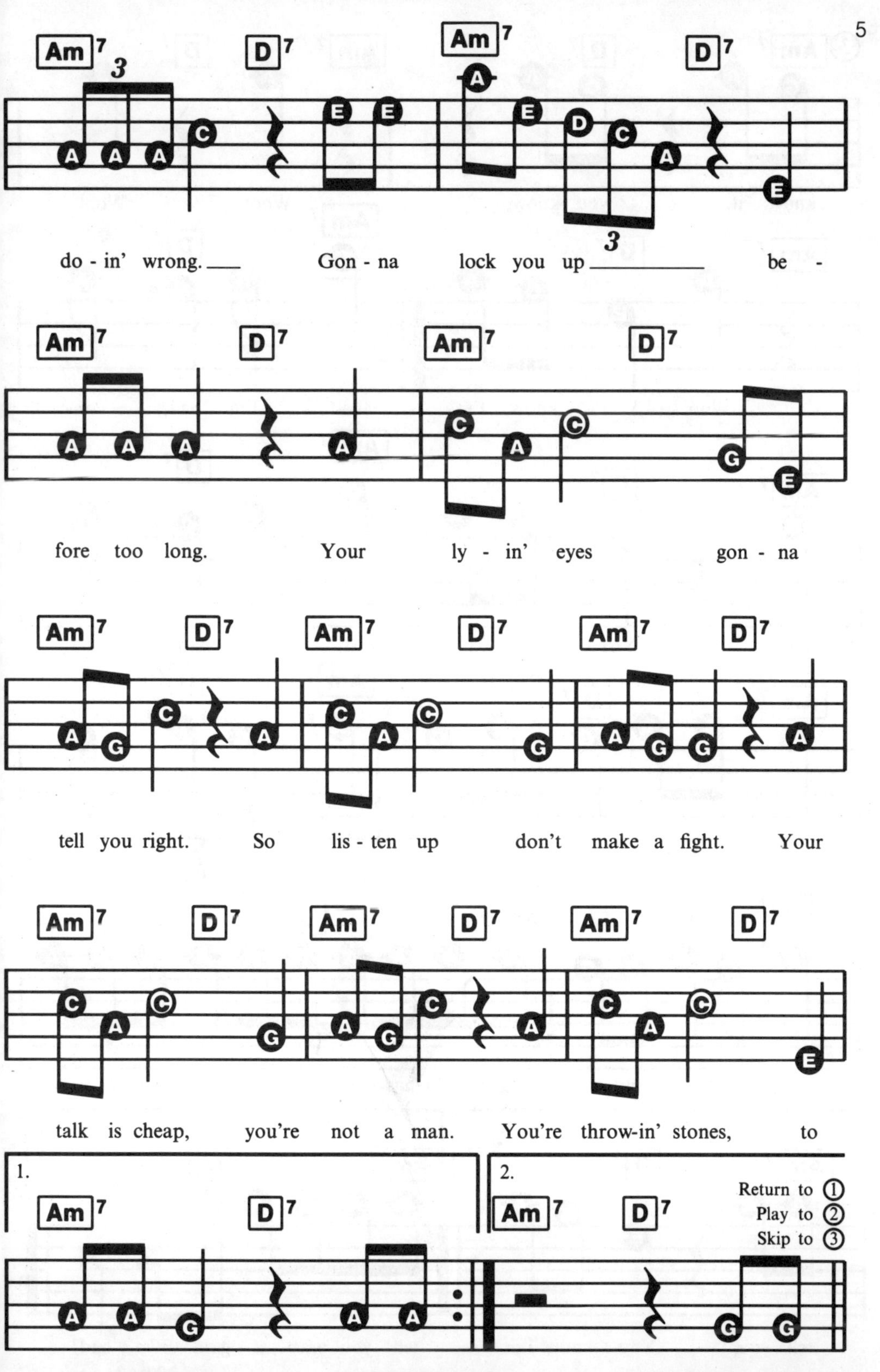
Am7 D7 Am7 D7
do - in' wrong. Gon - na lock you up be -
Am7 D7 Am7 D7
fore too long. Your ly - in' eyes gon - na
Am7 D7 Am7 D7 Am7 D7
tell you right. So lis - ten up don't make a fight. Your
Am7 D7 Am7 D7 Am7 D7
talk is cheap, you're not a man. You're throw-in' stones, to
1.
Am7 D7
hide your hands. But they
2.
Am7 D7
Return to ①
Play to ②
Skip to ③
We can

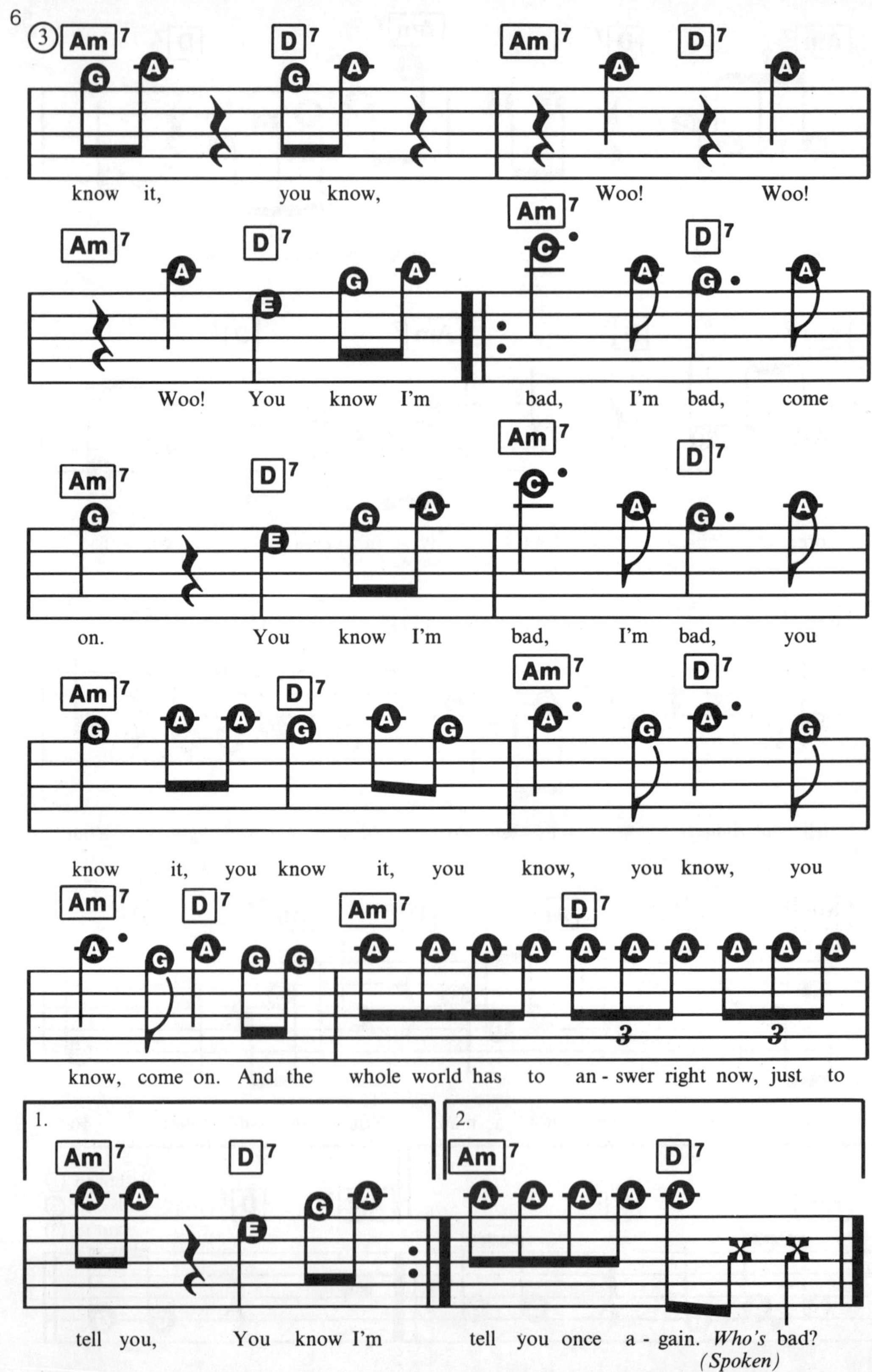
3
Am7 D7 Am7 D7
know it, you know, Woo! Woo!
Am7 D7 Am7 D7
Woo! You know I'm bad, I'm bad, come
Am7 D7 Am7 D7
on. You know I'm bad, I'm bad, you
Am7 D7 Am7 D7
know it, you know it, you know, you know, you
Am7 D7 Am7 D7
know, come on. And the whole world has to an - swer right now, just to
1. Am7 D7
tell you, You know I'm
2. Am7 D7
tell you once a - gain. Who's bad?
(Spoken)

ANOTHER PART OF ME

TROMBONE
BRIGHT 'N' BRASSY
Medium ROCK

Words and Music by
MICHAEL JACKSON

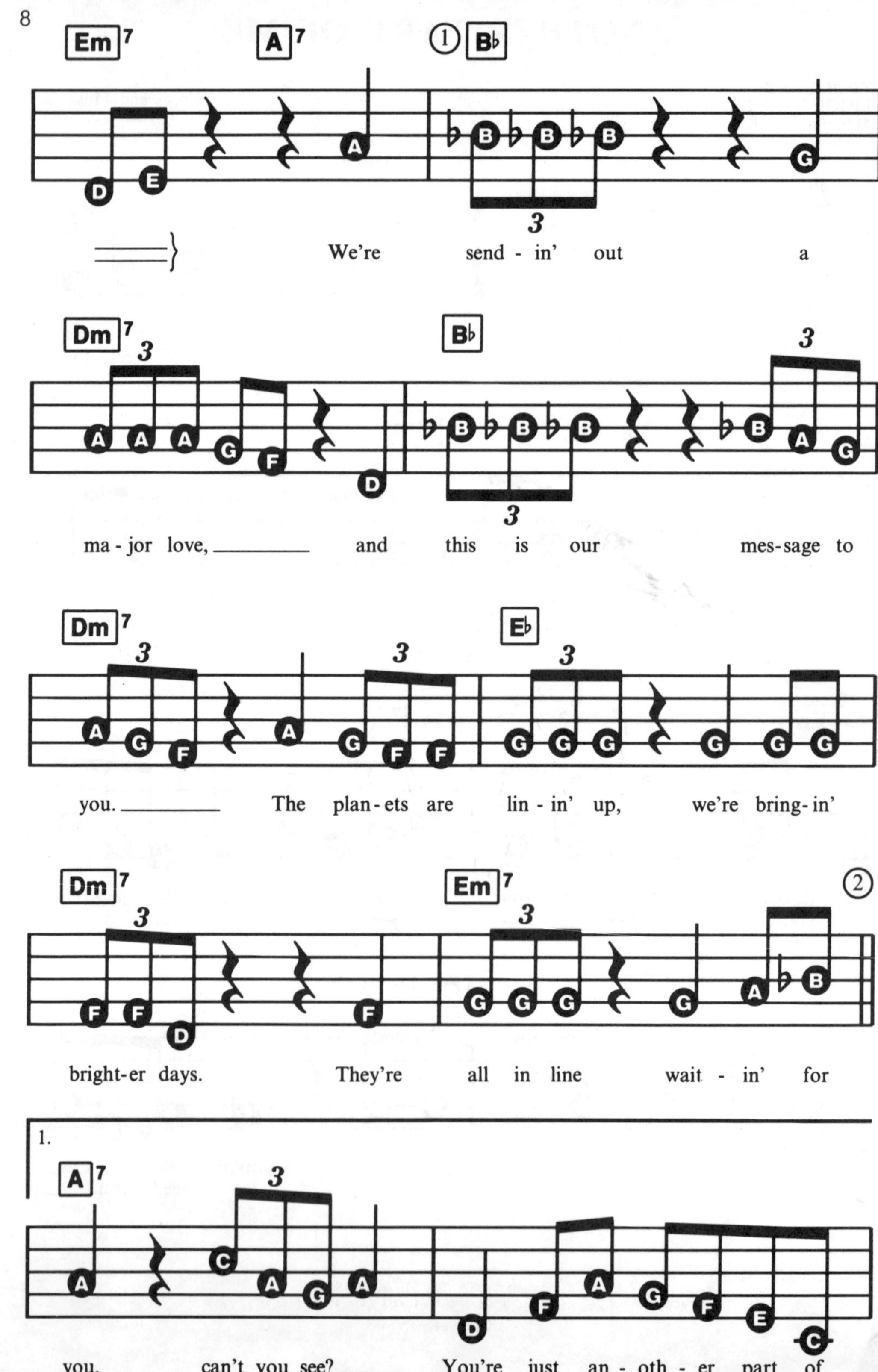
Em7 A7 ① B♭
We're send - in' out a
Dm7 B♭
ma - jor love, and this is our mes-sage to
Dm7 E♭
you. The plan - ets are lin - in' up, we're bring - in'
Dm7 Em7 ②
bright-er days. They're all in line wait - in' for
1.
A7
you, can't you see? You're just an - oth - er part of

Dm — Cm7

me, hee hee! Ooh!

Em7 A7 — 2. A7

Out from a na - you sho' nuff true. ______

Dm

You're just an - oth - er part of me, hee hee! Ooh!

Cm7 Em7 A7

Return to ①
Play to ②
Skip to ③

③ A7

We're you, Can't you see? ______

Dm7

You're just an - oth - er part of me, hee

Cm7 Em7 A7 Repeat and fade

hee! Ooh! An - oth - er part of

BILLIE JEAN

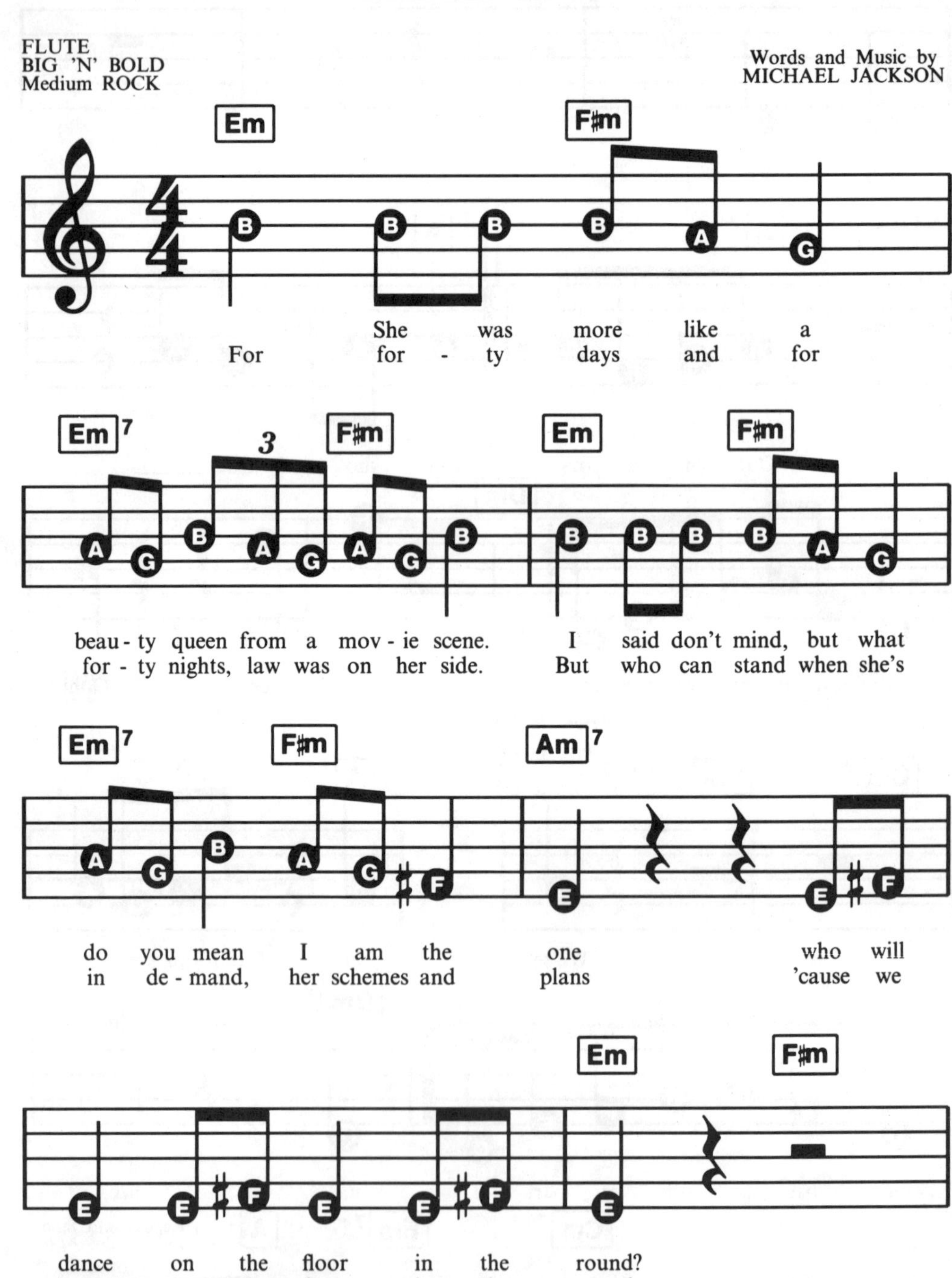
FLUTE
BIG 'N' BOLD
Medium ROCK
Words and Music by
MICHAEL JACKSON
Em
F♯m
She was more like a
For for - ty days and for
Em7
3
F♯m
Em
F♯m
beau - ty queen from a mov - ie scene. I said don't mind, but what
for - ty nights, law was on her side. But who can stand when she's
Em7
F♯m
Am7
do you mean I am the one who will
in de - mand, her schemes and plans 'cause we
Em
F♯m
dance on the floor in the round?
danced on the floor in the round.

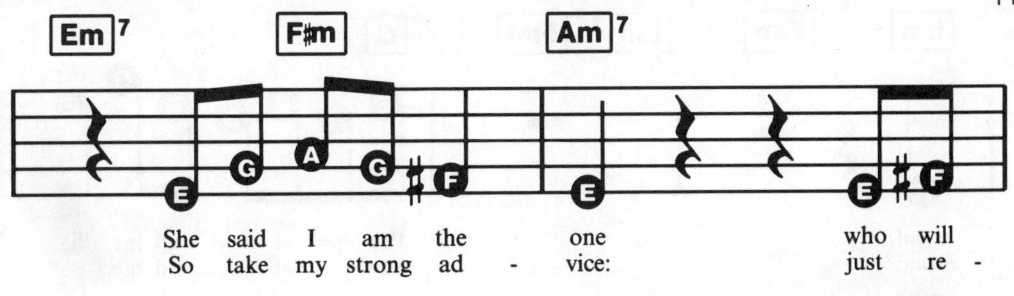
Em7
F#m
Am7
E G A G #F
E
E #F
She said I am the one who will
So take my strong ad - vice: just re -

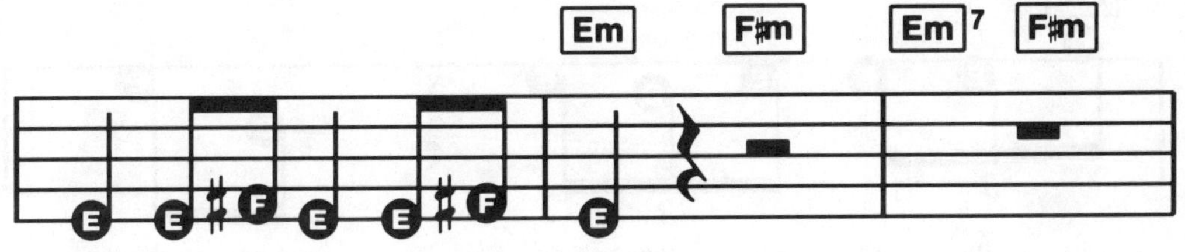
Em
F#m
Em7
F#m
E E #F E E #F E
dance on the floor in the round.
mem - ber to al - ways think twice.

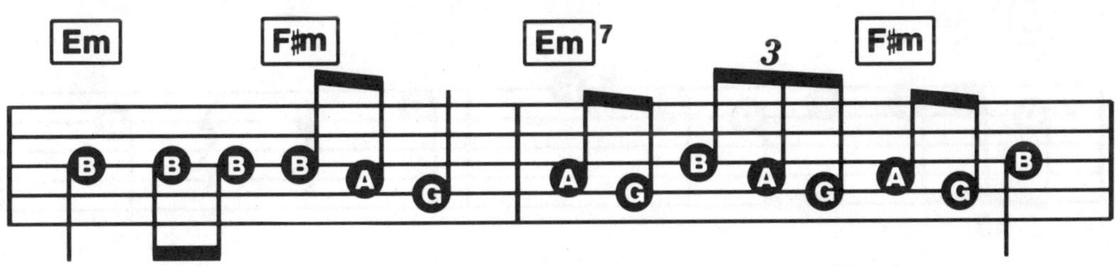
Em
F#m
Em7
F#m
3
B B B B A G A G B A G A G B
She told me her name was Bil - lie Jean and she caused a scene.
She told me ba - by we danced til three, and she looked at me,

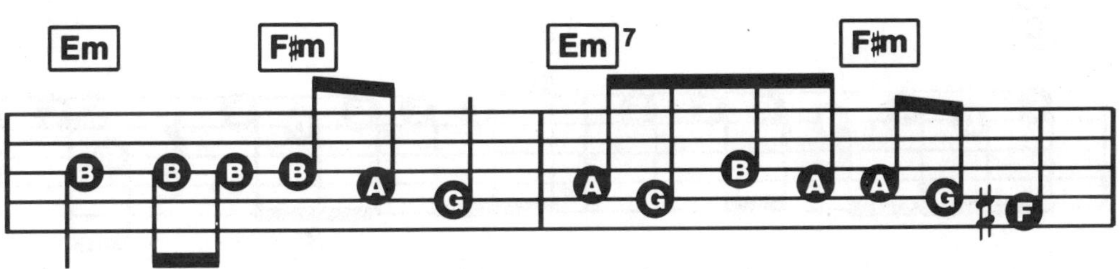
Em
F#m
Em7
F#m
B B B B A G A G B A A G #F
Then ev - 'ry head turned with eyes that dreamed of be - ing the
then showed a pho - to. My ba - by cried. His eyes were like

Am7

E E #F E E #F E E #F
one who will dance on the floor in the
mine. Can we dance on the floor in the

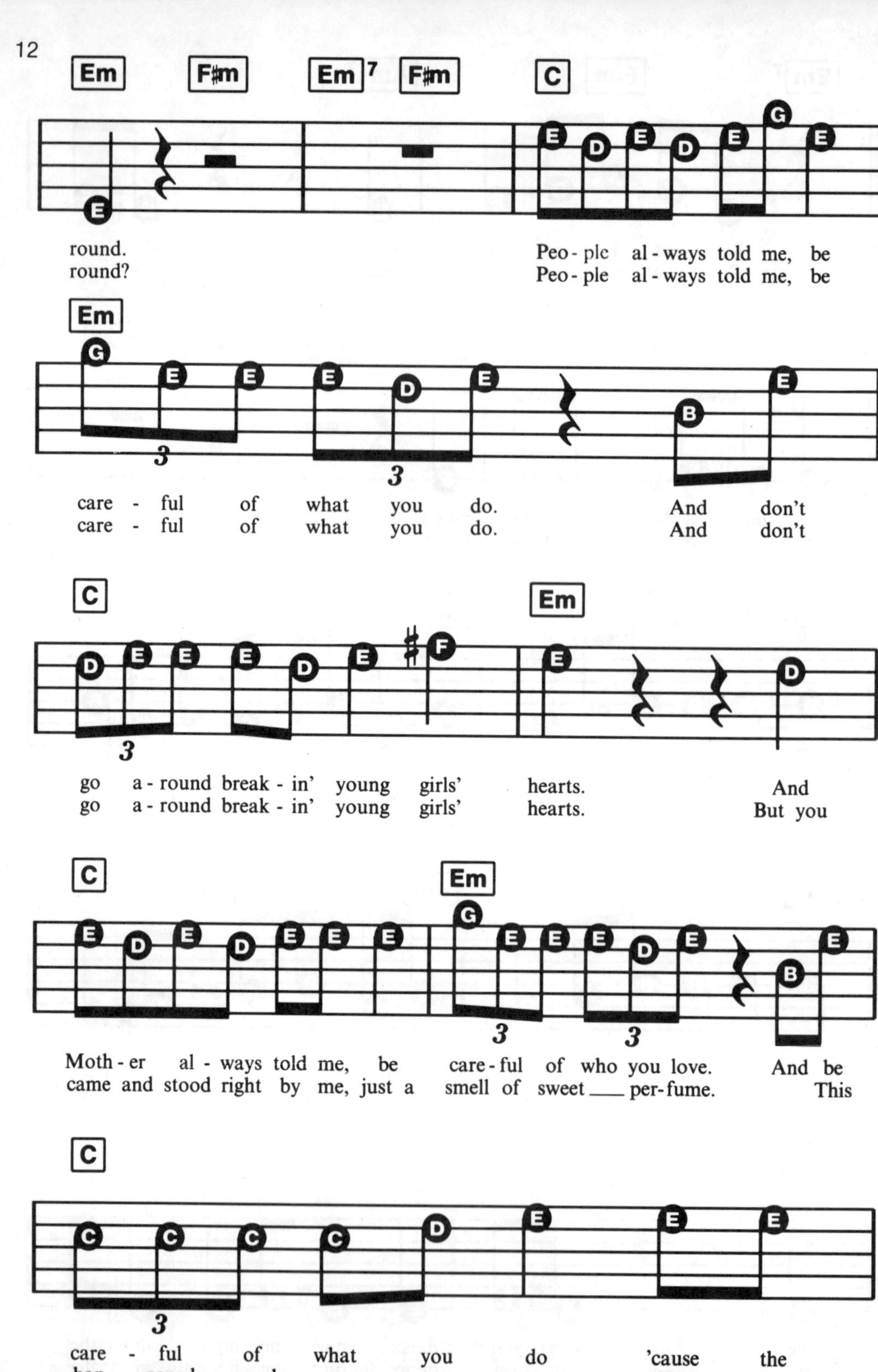
Em F#m Em7 F#m C
round.
round?
Peo - ple al - ways told me, be
Peo - ple al - ways told me, be
Em
care - ful of what you do. And don't
care - ful of what you do. And don't
C Em
go a - round break - in' young girls' hearts. And
go a - round break - in' young girls' hearts. But you
C Em
Moth - er al - ways told me, be care - ful of who you love. And be
came and stood right by me, just a smell of sweet ___ per - fume. This
C
care - ful of what you do 'cause the
hap - pened much ______ too soon. She ______

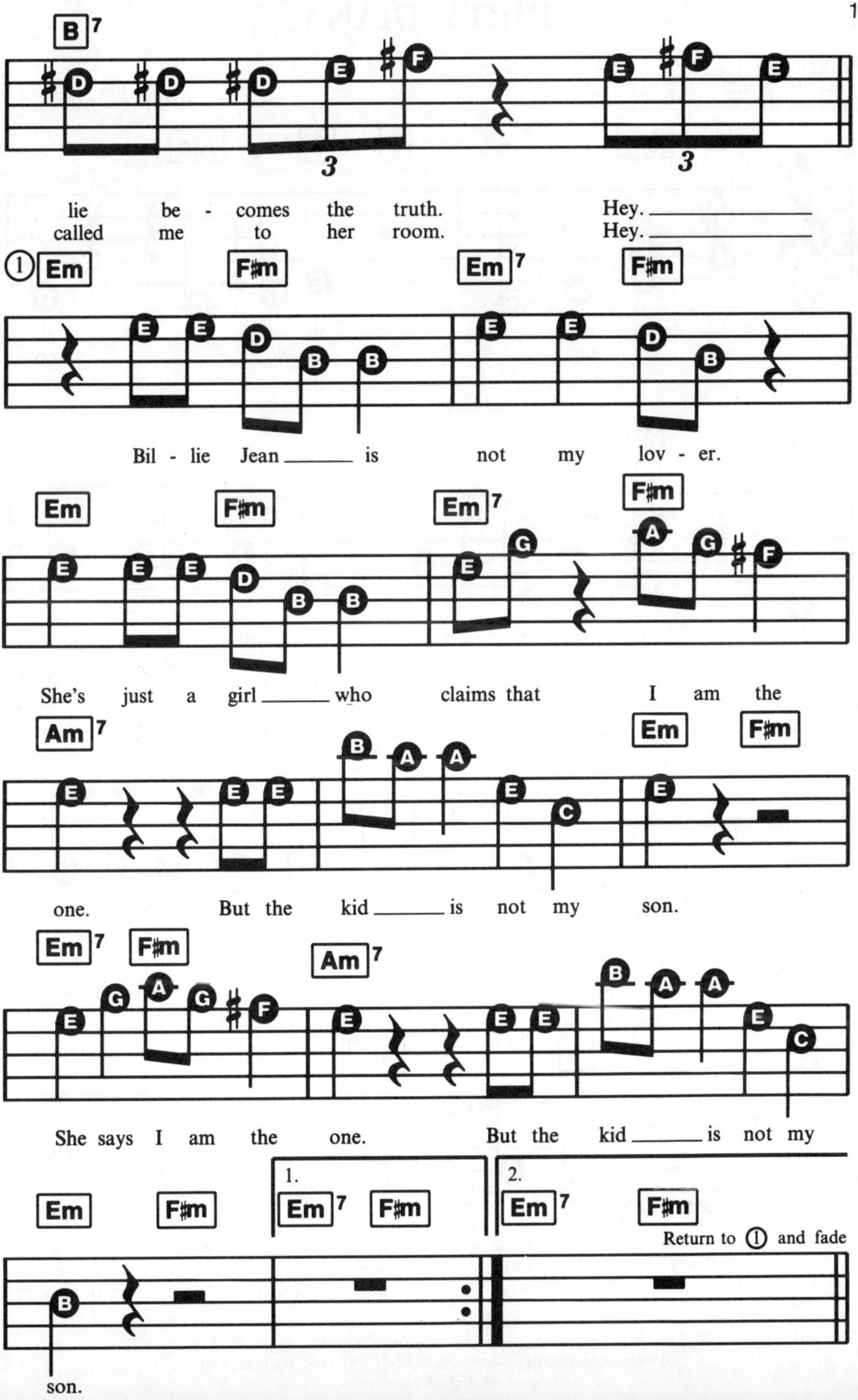

B7

lie be - comes the truth. Hey. ______
called me to her room. Hey. ______

① Em F♯m Em7 F♯m

Bil - lie Jean ______ is not my lov - er.

Em F♯m Em7 F♯m

She's just a girl ______ who claims that I am the

Am7 Em F♯m

one. But the kid ______ is not my son.

Em7 F♯m Am7

She says I am the one. But the kid ______ is not my ______

Em F♯m 1. Em7 F♯m 2. Em7 F♯m

Return to ① and fade

son.

DIRTY DIANA

SAXOPHONE
BIG 'N' BOLD
Medium ROCK
Words and Music by
MICHAEL JACKSON
1
Am F G Am
Oh no, oh no, oh
Oh no, oh no, oh
F G Am
no. You'll nev - er make me stay so take your
no. She likes the boys in the band, she knows when
She said I have to go home, 'cause I'm real
F G Am
weight off of me. I know your ev - 'ry move, so won't you
they come to town. Ev - 'ry mu - si - cian's fan af - ter the
tired, you see. But I hate sleep - in' alone. Why don't you
F G Am
just let me be. I've been here times be - fore, but I was
cur - tain comes down. She waits at back - stage doors for those who
come with me? I said my ba - by's at home she's prob - ably

F G Am

too blind to see that you se - duce ev' - ry man. This time you
have pres - tige, who prom - ise for - tune and fame, a life that's
wor - ried to - night. I did - n't call on the phone to say that

F G Am

won't se - duce me. She's say - ing that's O. K. Hey, ba - by
so care - free. She's say - ing that's O. K. Hey, ba - by
I'm al - right. ____ Di - an - a walked up to me. She said I'm

F G Am

do what you please. I have the stuff that you want. I am the
do what you want. I'll be your night lov - in' thing, I'll be the
all yours to - night. At that I ran to the phone say - in' ba -

F G Am

thing that you need. She looked me deep in the eyes. She's touch - in'
freak you can taunt. And I don't care what you say, I want to
by, I'm al - right. I said, but un - lock the door be - cause I

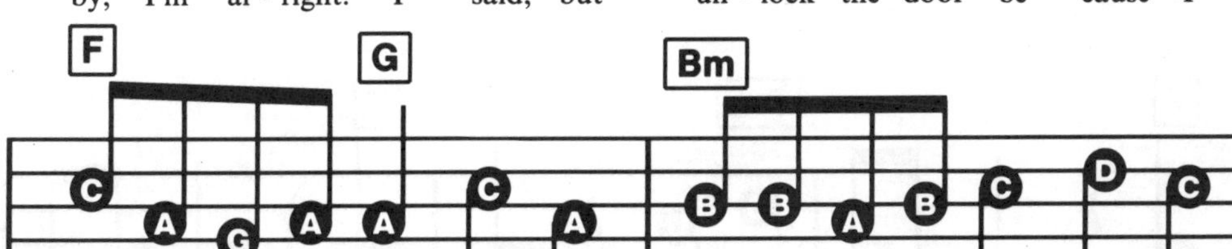

me so to start. She says there's no turn - in' back. She trapped me
go too ____ far. I'll be your ev - 'ry - thing if you make
for - got the key. She said he's not com - ing back, be - cause he's

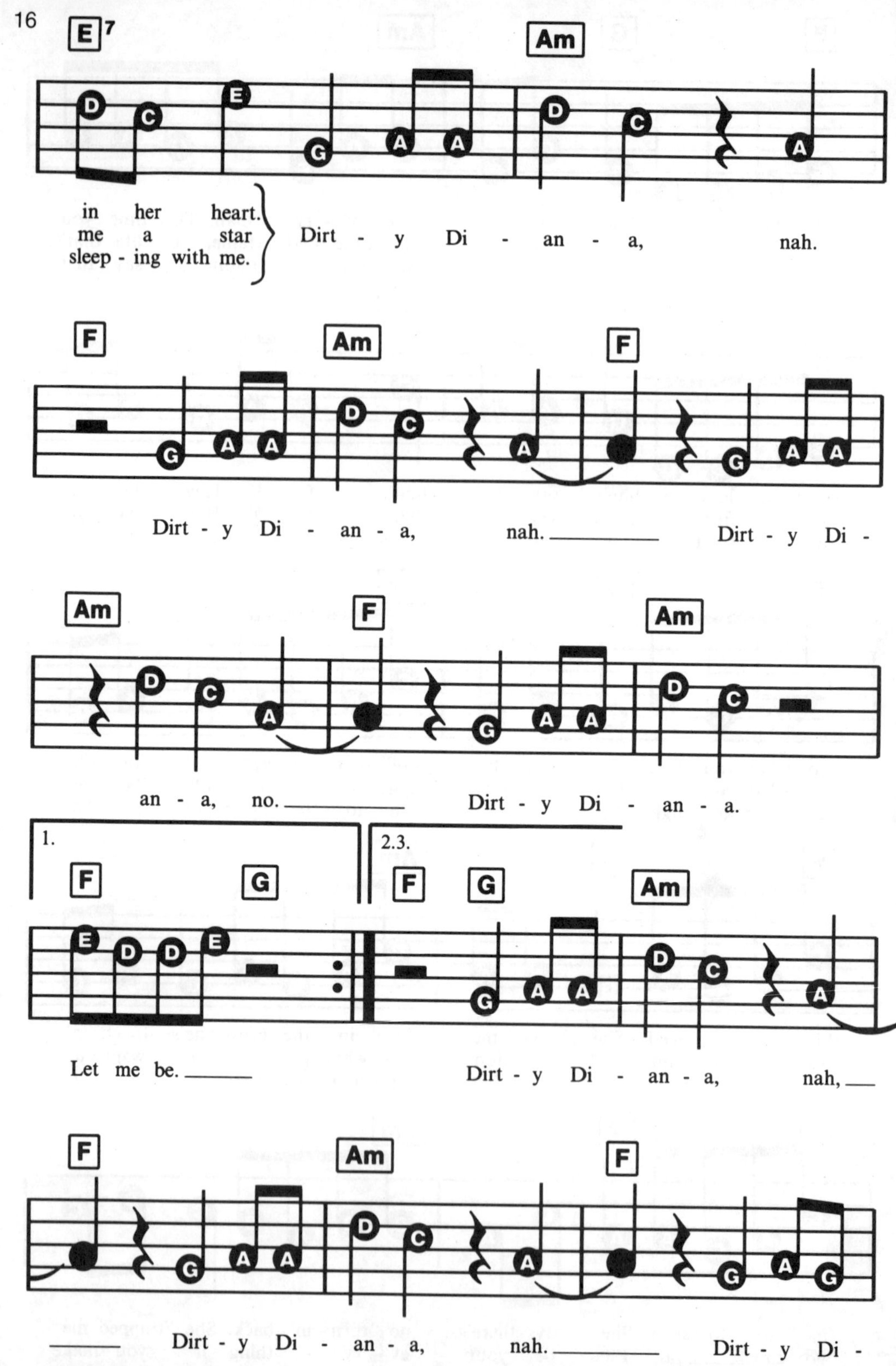
E7 Am
in her heart. / me a star / sleep - ing with me.
Dirt - y Di - an - a, nah.
F Am F
Dirt - y Di - an - a, nah. Dirt - y Di -
Am F Am
an - a, no. Dirt - y Di - an - a.
1. F G
Let me be.
2.3. F G Am
Dirt - y Di - an - a, nah,
F Am F
Dirt - y Di - an - a, nah. Dirt - y Di -

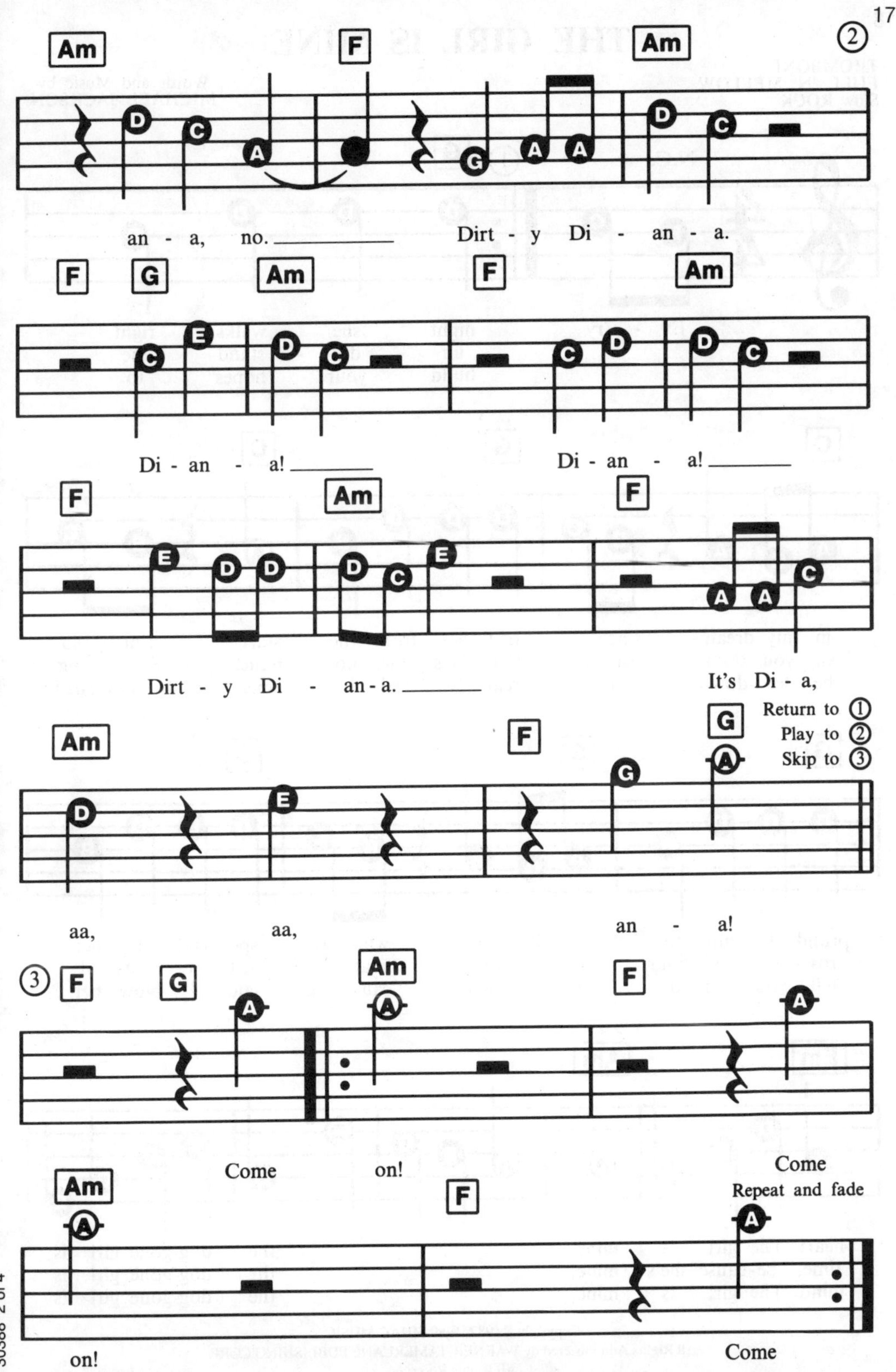
②
Am
F
Am
D
C
A
G
A
A
D
C
an - a, no.
Dirt - y Di - an - a.
F
G
Am
F
Am
E
C
D
C
C
D
D
C
Di - an - a!
Di - an - a!
F
Am
F
E
D
D
D
C
E
A
A
C
Dirt - y Di - an - a.
It's Di - a,
Return to ①
Play to ②
Skip to ③
Am
F
G
D
E
G
A
aa,
aa,
an - a!
③
F
G
Am
F
A
A
A
Come
on!
Come
Repeat and fade
Am
F
A
A
on!
Come

THE GIRL IS MINE

TROMBONE
FULL 'N' MELLOW
Slow ROCK

Words and Music by
MICHAEL JACKSON

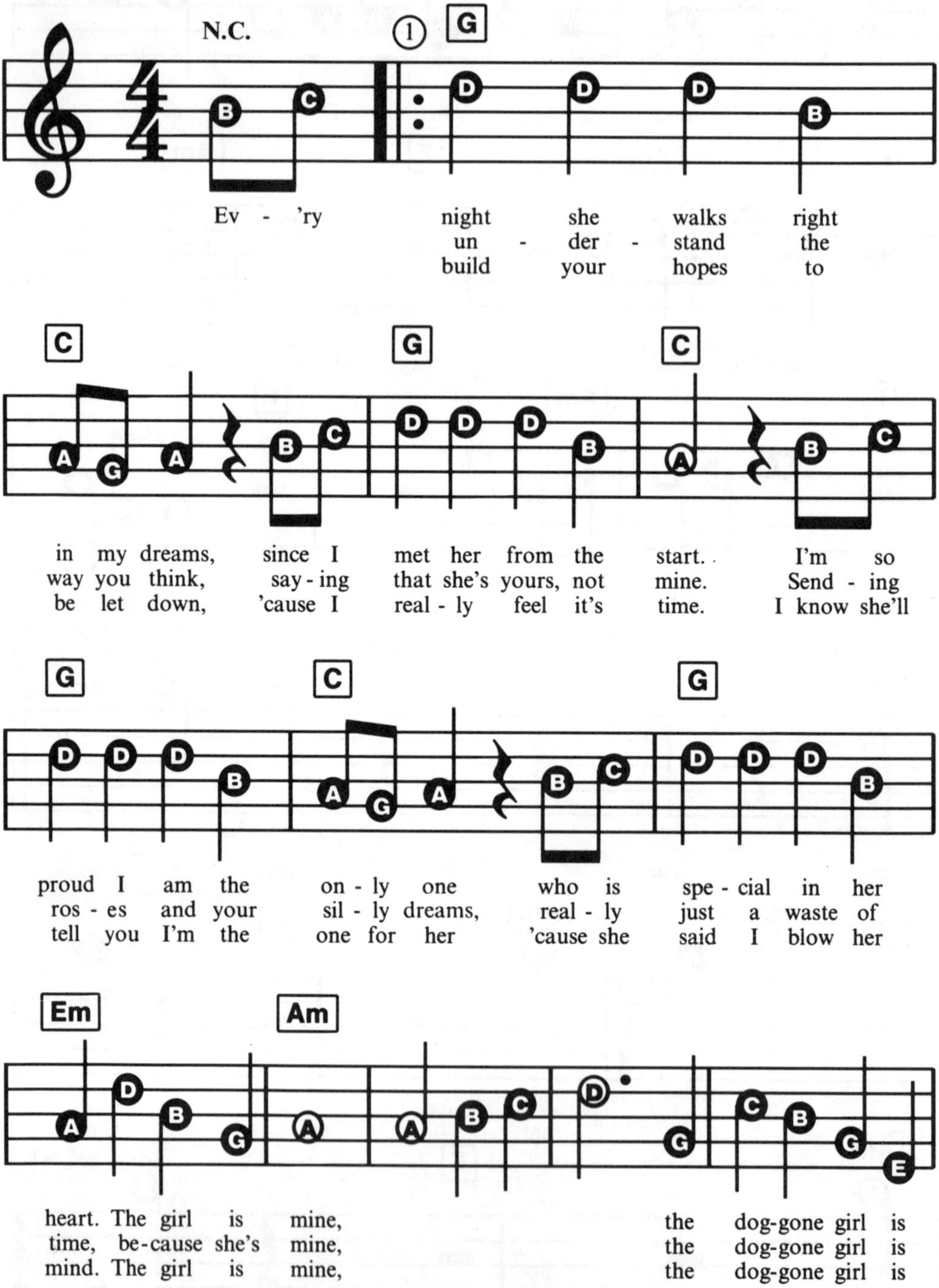

N.C. ① G

B C | D D D B

Ev - 'ry | night she walks right
un - der - stand the
build your hopes to

C G C

A G A B C | D D D B | A B C

in my dreams, since I | met her from the | start. I'm so
way you think, say - ing | that she's yours, not | mine. Send - ing
be let down, 'cause I | real - ly feel it's | time. I know she'll

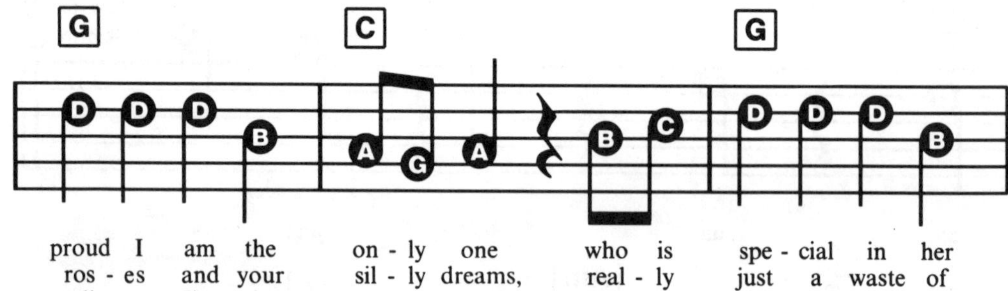

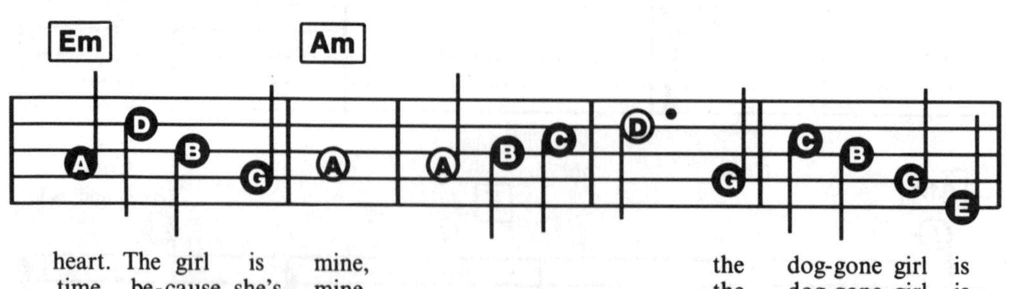

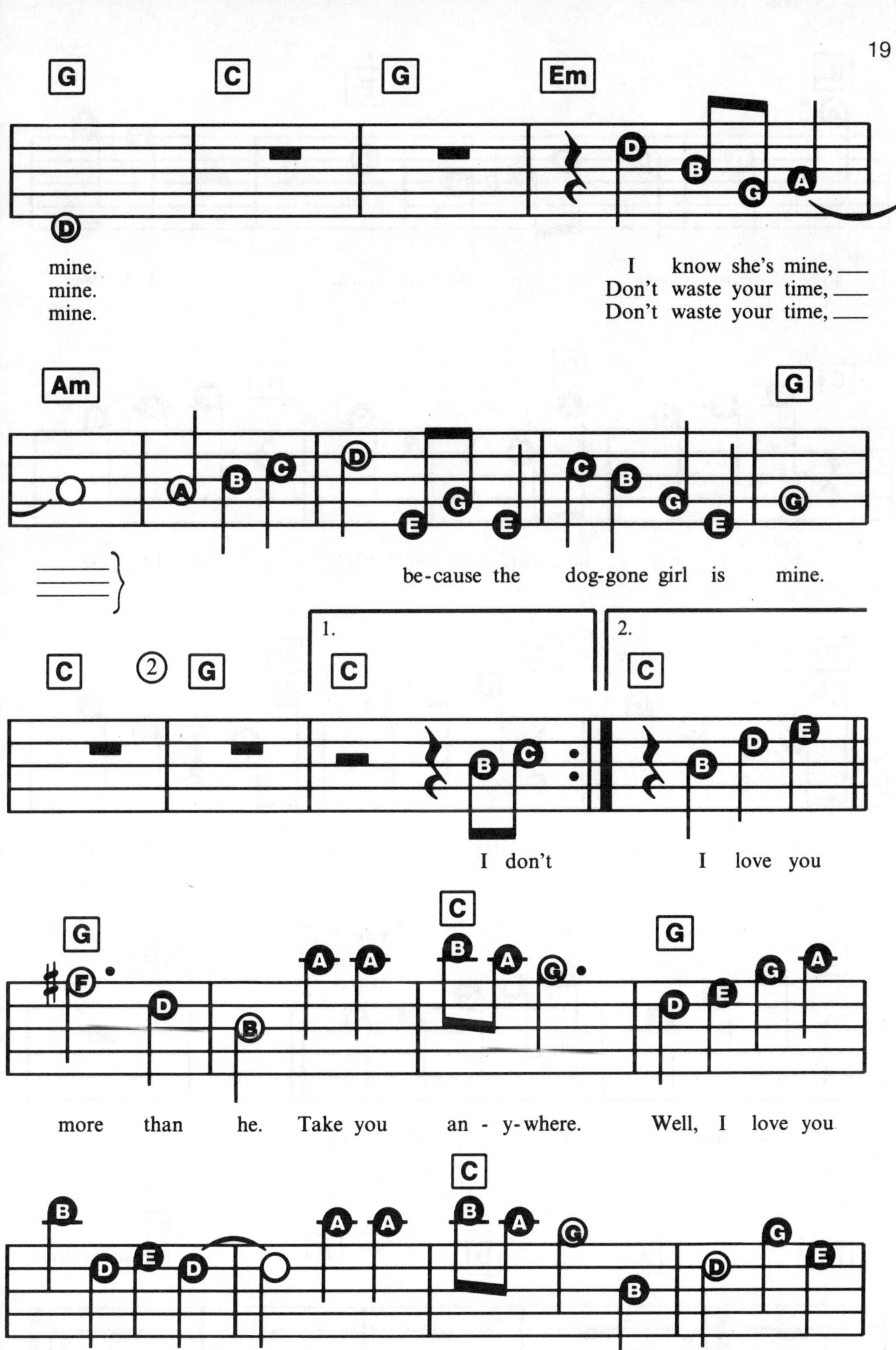
G C G Em
mine. I know she's mine, ___
mine. Don't waste your time, ___
mine. Don't waste your time, ___
Am G
be-cause the dog-gone girl is mine.
C 2 G
1. C
2. C
I don't
I love you
G C G
more than he. Take you an - y-where. Well, I love you
C
end-less-ly ___ lov - ing we will share. So come and ___

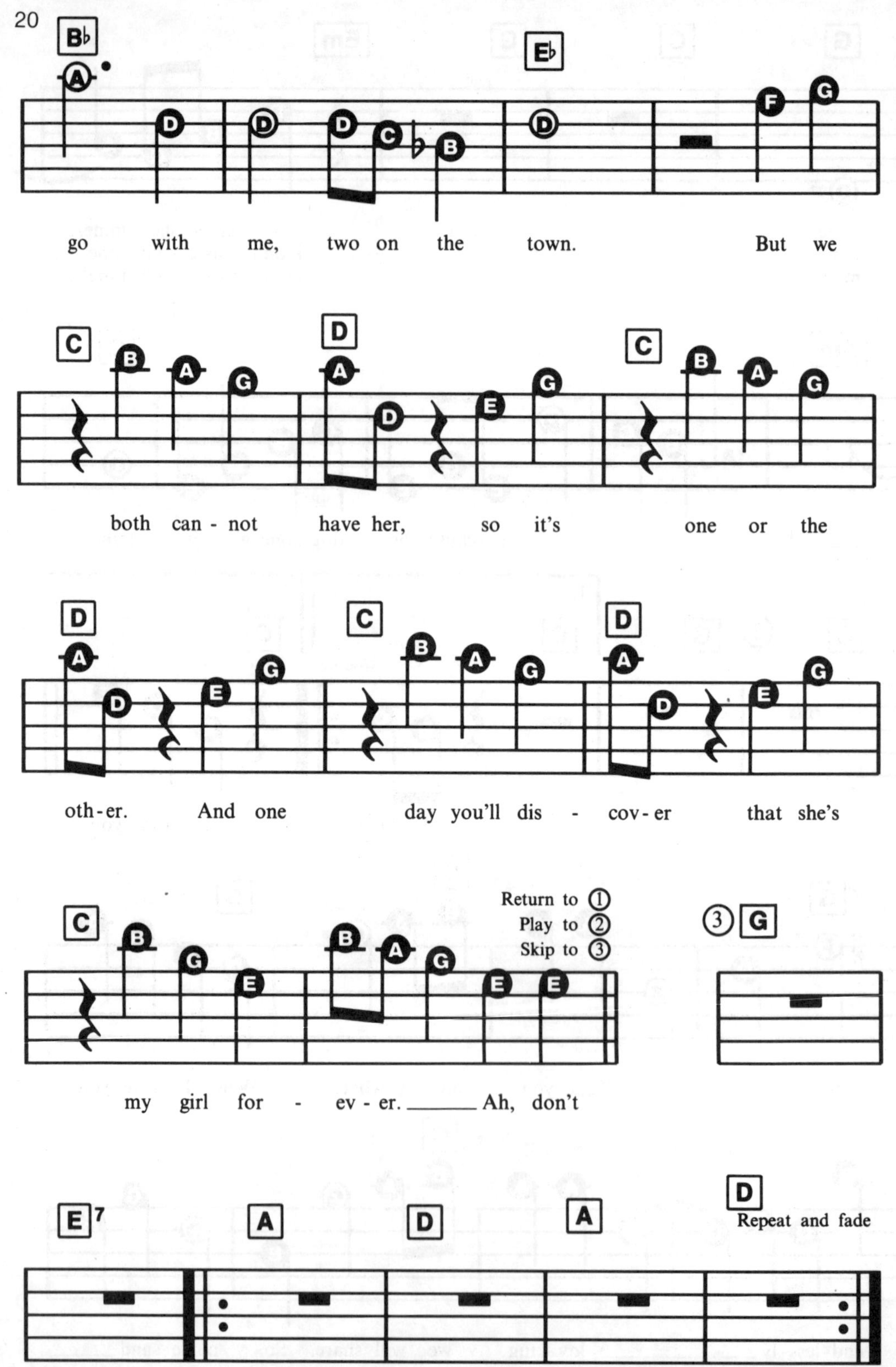
B♭
E♭
go with me, two on the town. But we
C
D
C
both can - not have her, so it's one or the
D
C
D
oth - er. And one day you'll dis - cov - er that she's
C
Return to ①
Play to ②
Skip to ③
③ G
my girl for - ev - er. ______ Ah, don't
E7
A
D
A
D
Repeat and fade

BEAT IT

GUITAR
BIG 'N' BOLD
Medium ROCK

Words and Music by
MICHAEL JACKSON

C
D
A G E D E E E
F E D B D E
fire's ___ in their eyes and their words are real - ly clear. So
wan - na stay a - live; bet - ter do what you ___ can. So

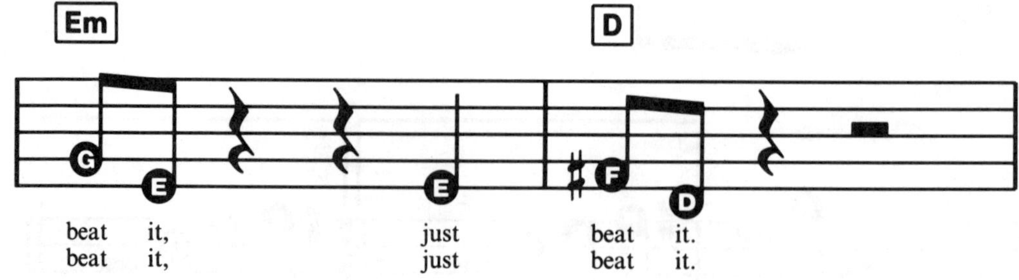
Em
D
G E E
F D
beat it, just beat it.
beat it, just beat it.

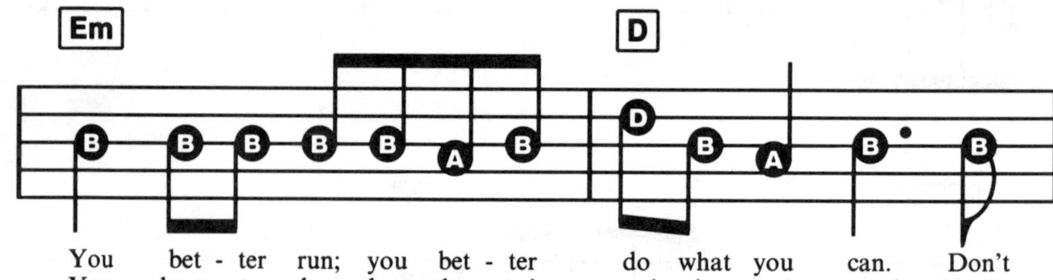
Em
D
B B B B B A B
D B A B B
You bet - ter run; you bet - ter do what you can. Don't
You have to show them that you're real - ly not scared. You're

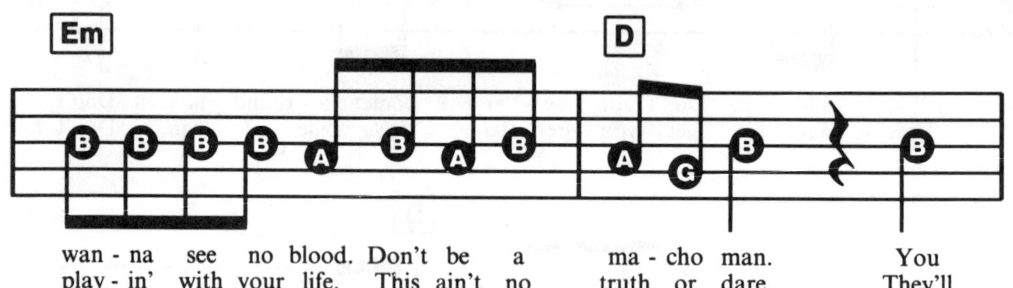
Em
D
B B B B A B A B
A G B B
wan - na see no blood. Don't be a ma - cho man. You
play - in' with your life. This ain't no truth or dare. They'll

C
D
A G E E E E
F E D D E
wan - na be tough; bet - ter do what you can. So
kick you, then they beat you, then they'll tell you it's fair. So

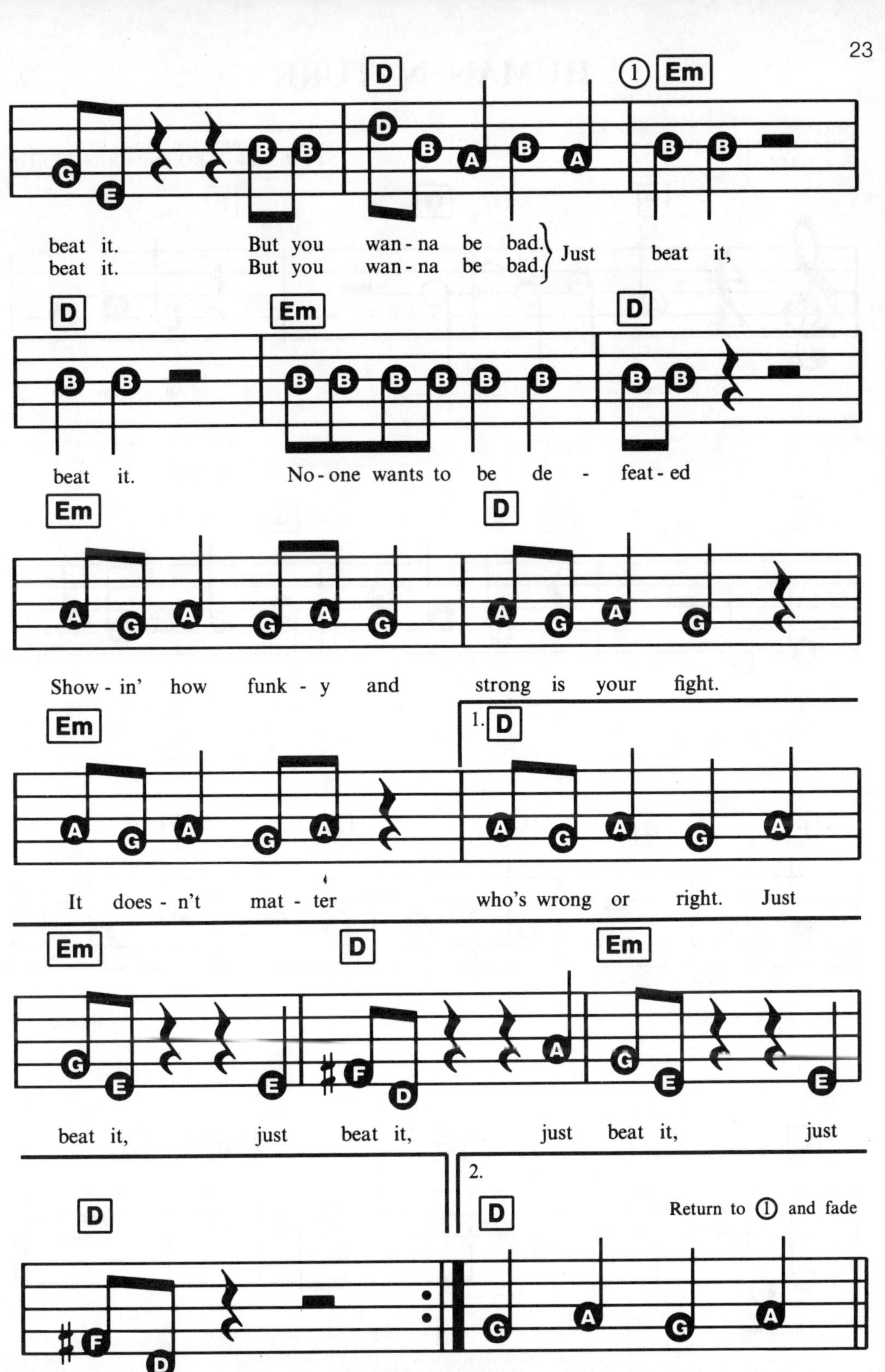
D
① Em
beat it. But you wan - na be bad.
beat it. But you wan - na be bad.
Just beat it,
D
Em
D
beat it. No - one wants to be de - feat - ed
Em
D
Show - in' how funk - y and strong is your fight.
Em
1. D
It does - n't mat - ter who's wrong or right. Just
Em
D
Em
beat it, just beat it, just beat it, just
D
2.
D
Return to ① and fade
beat it. wrong or right. Just

HUMAN NATURE

ORGAN
FULL 'N' MELLOW
Fast BALLAD

Words and Music by
STEVE PORCARO and JOHN BETTIS

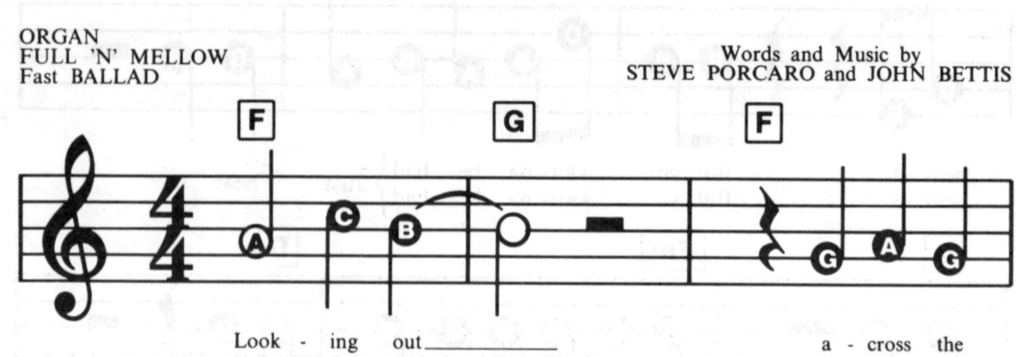

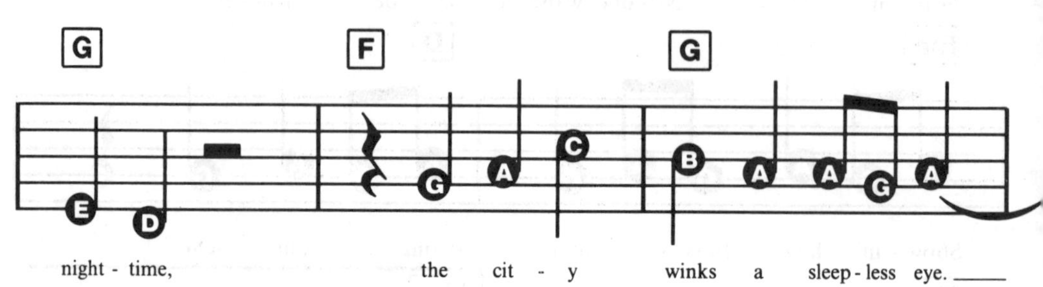

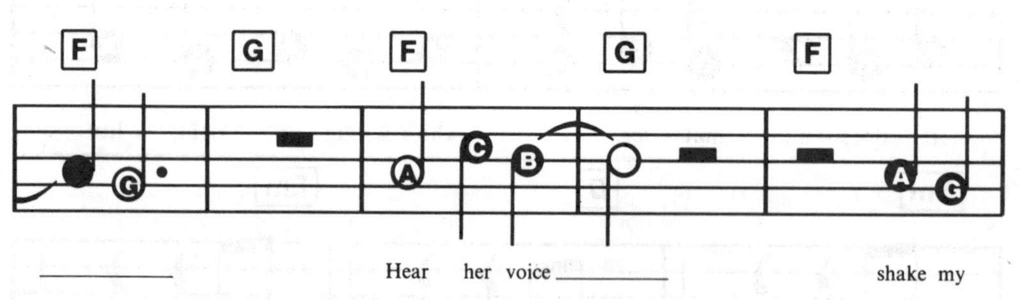

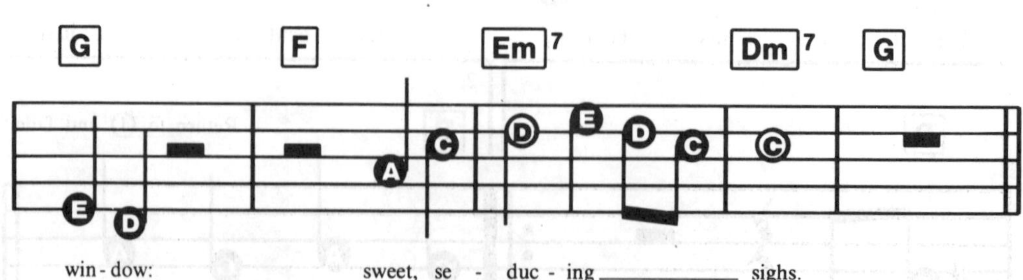

①

F | G | F | G

A C B (tied) B — | rest G A G | E D rest

Get me out ______ into the night-time.
Reach - ing out ______ to touch a stran - ger,
Look - ing out ______ a - cross the morn - ing,

F | G | F | G

rest G A C | B A G A (tied) G. | rest

Four walls won't hold me to - night. ______
e - lec - tric eyes are ev'ry-where, ______
the cit - y's heart begins to beat. ______

F | G | F | G

A C B (tied) B — | rest G A G | E D rest

If this town ______ is just an ap - ple,
See that girl? ______ She know's I'm watch - ing.
Reach - ing out, ______ I touch her shoul - der.

F | Em7 | Dm7 | G

rest G A C | D E D C | C | rest G A G

then let me take a ______ bite.
She likes the way I ______ stare.
I'm dream - ing of the ______ street.

If they say,

F | G | C | Am7

A rest rest B | rest | E D C B | C B A G

"Why, why?" tell 'em that it's hu - man na - ture.

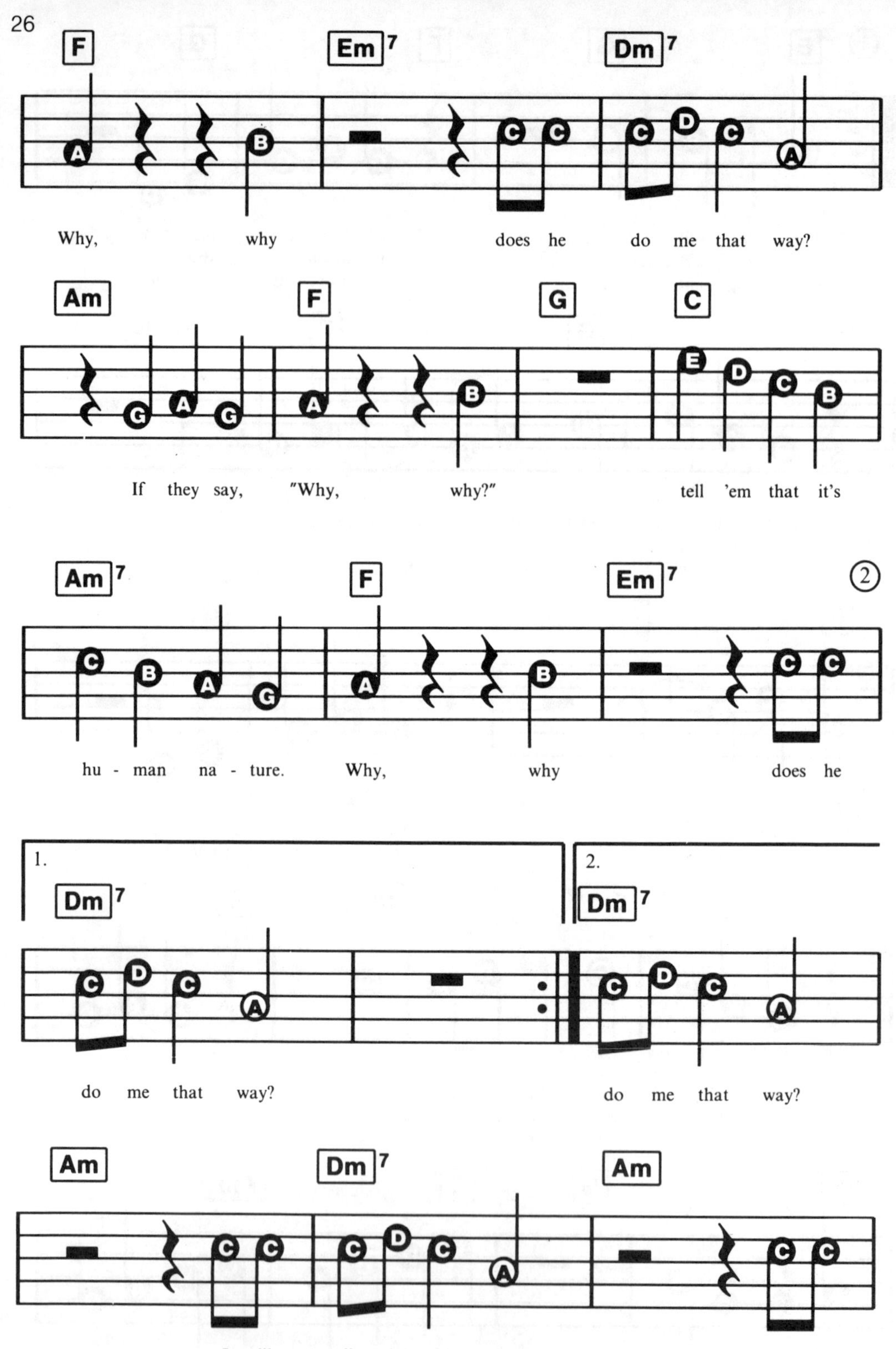
F
Em7
Dm7
Why, why does he do me that way?
Am
F
G
C
If they say, "Why, why?" tell 'em that it's
Am7
F
Em7
2
hu - man na - ture. Why, why does he
1.
Dm7
do me that way?
2.
Dm7
do me that way?
Am
Dm7
Am
I like liv - in' this way I like

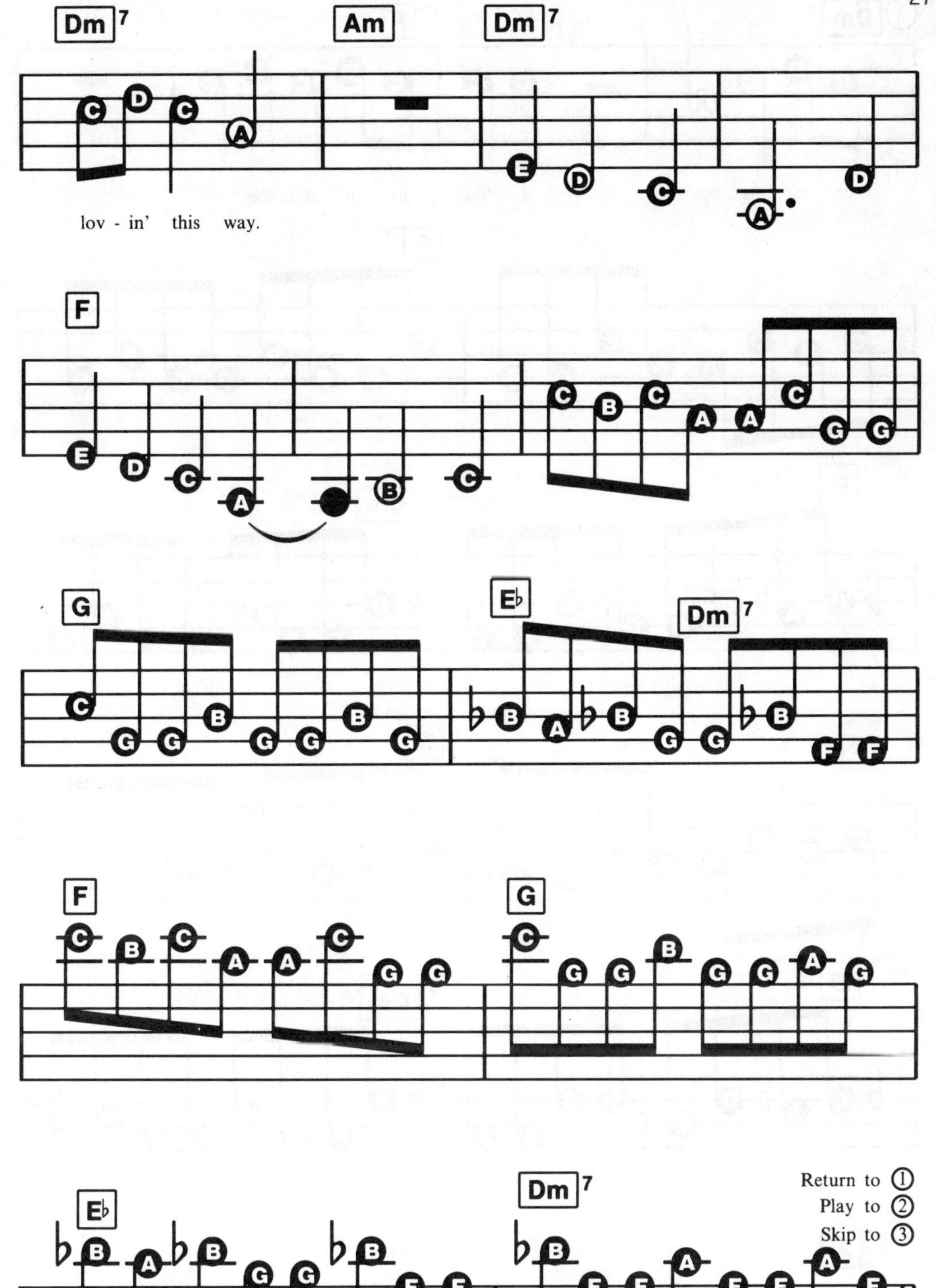
Dm7
Am
Dm7
lov - in' this way.
F
G
E♭
Dm7
F
G
E♭
Dm7
Return to ①
Play to ②
Skip to ③

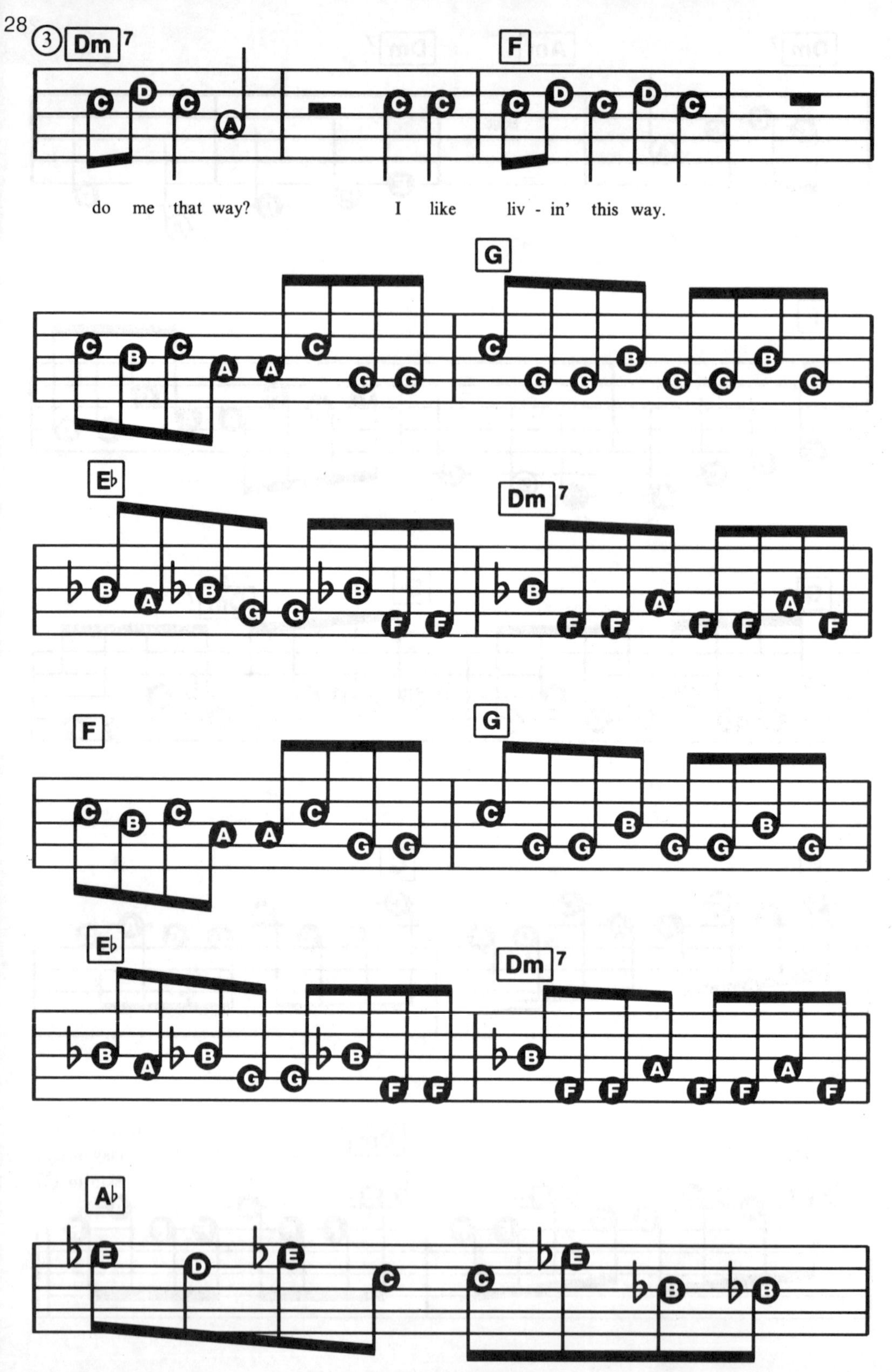
3
Dm7
F
C D C A
C C
C D C D C
do me that way?
I like
liv - in' this way.
G
C B C A A C G G
C G G B G G B G
E♭
Dm7
B A B G G B F F
B F F A F F A F
F
G
C B C A A C G G
C G G B G G B G
E♭
Dm7
B A B G G B F F
B F F A F F A F
A♭
E D E C
C E B B

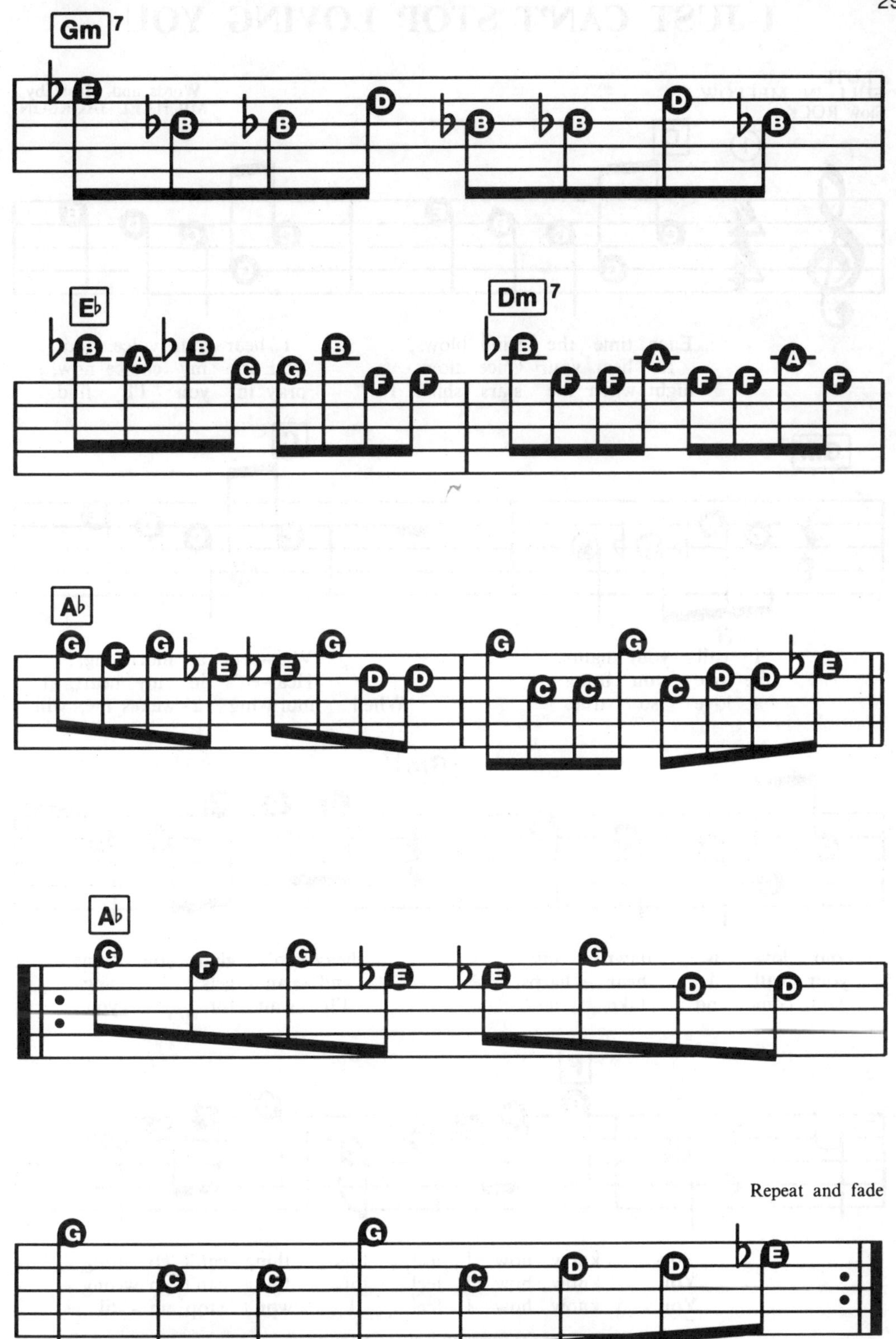
Gm7
E♭
Dm7
A♭
A♭
Repeat and fade

I JUST CAN'T STOP LOVING YOU

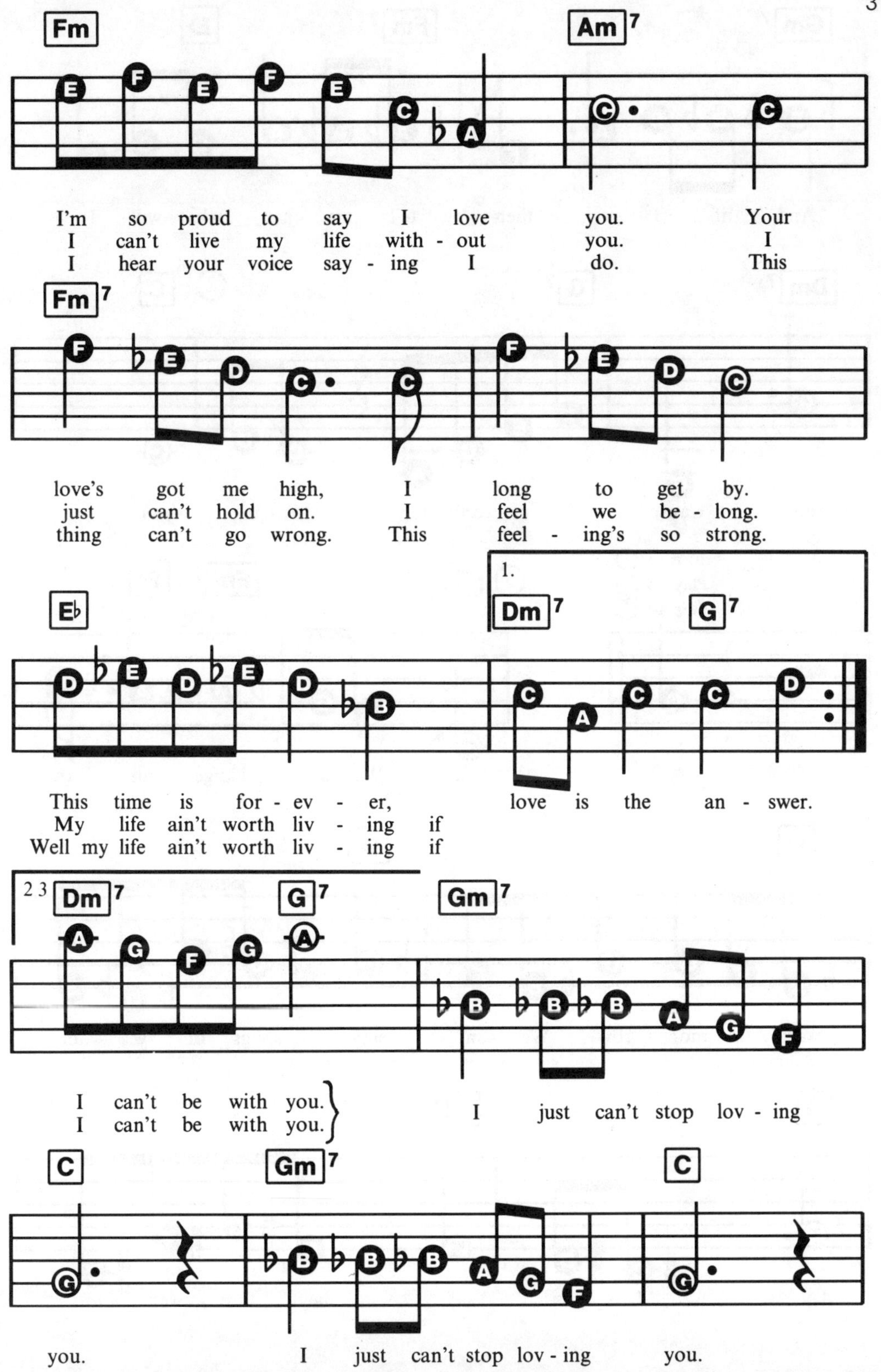
Fm
Am7
I'm so proud to say I love you. Your
I can't live my life with - out you. I
I hear your voice say - ing I do. This
Fm7
love's got me high, I long to get by.
just can't hold on. I feel we be - long.
thing can't go wrong. This feel - ing's so strong.
1.
Eb
Dm7
G7
This time is for - ev - er, love is the an - swer.
My life ain't worth liv - ing if
Well my life ain't worth liv - ing if
2 3
Dm7
G7
Gm7
I can't be with you.
I can't be with you.
I just can't stop lov - ing
C
Gm7
C
you. I just can't stop lov - ing you.

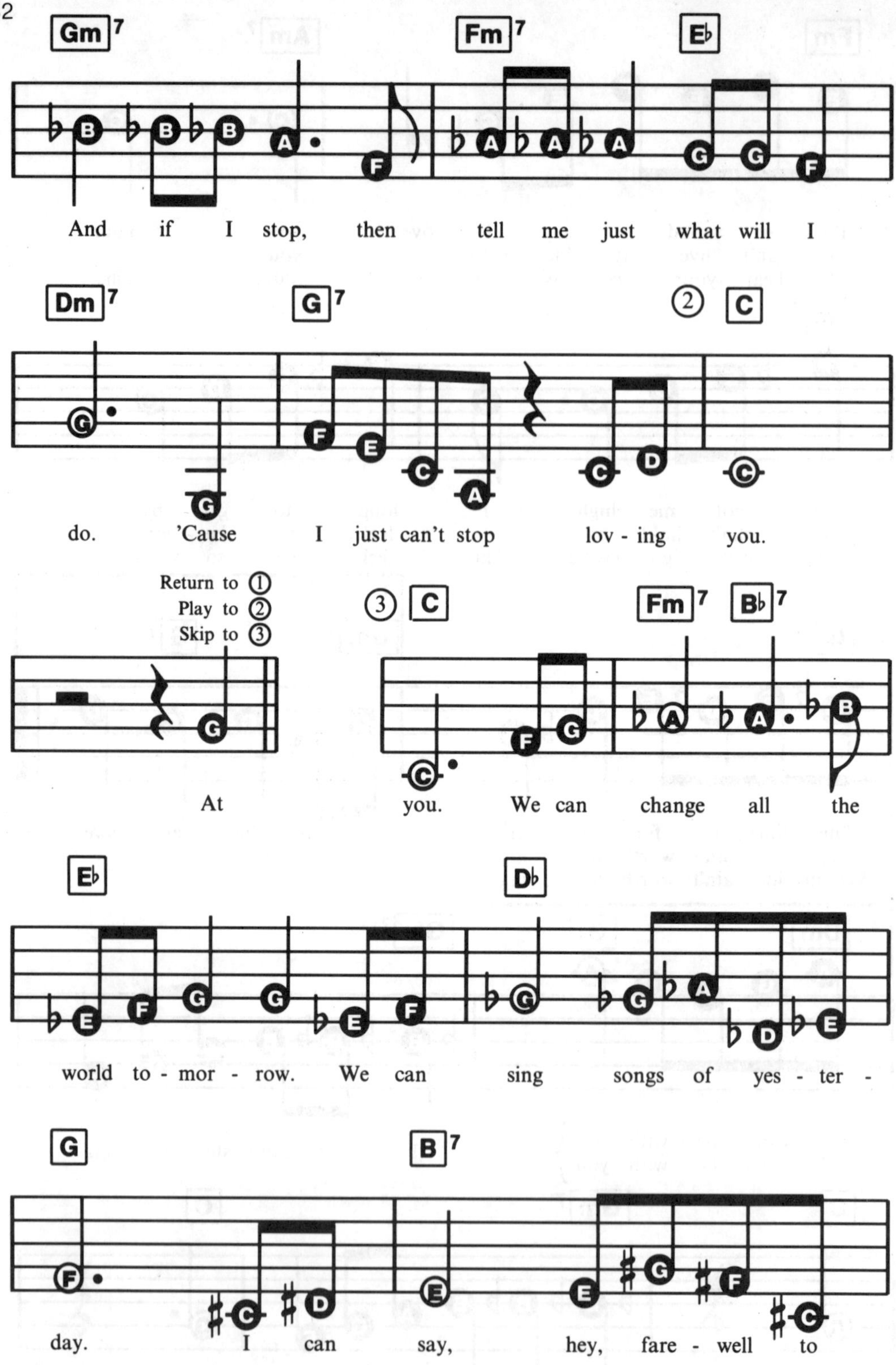

Gm7 Fm7 E♭

And if I stop, then tell me just what will I

Dm7 G7 ② C

do. 'Cause I just can't stop lov - ing you.

Return to ①
Play to ②
Skip to ③

③ C Fm7 B♭7

At you. We can change all the

E♭ D♭

world to - mor - row. We can sing songs of yes - ter -

G B7

day. I can say, hey, fare - well to

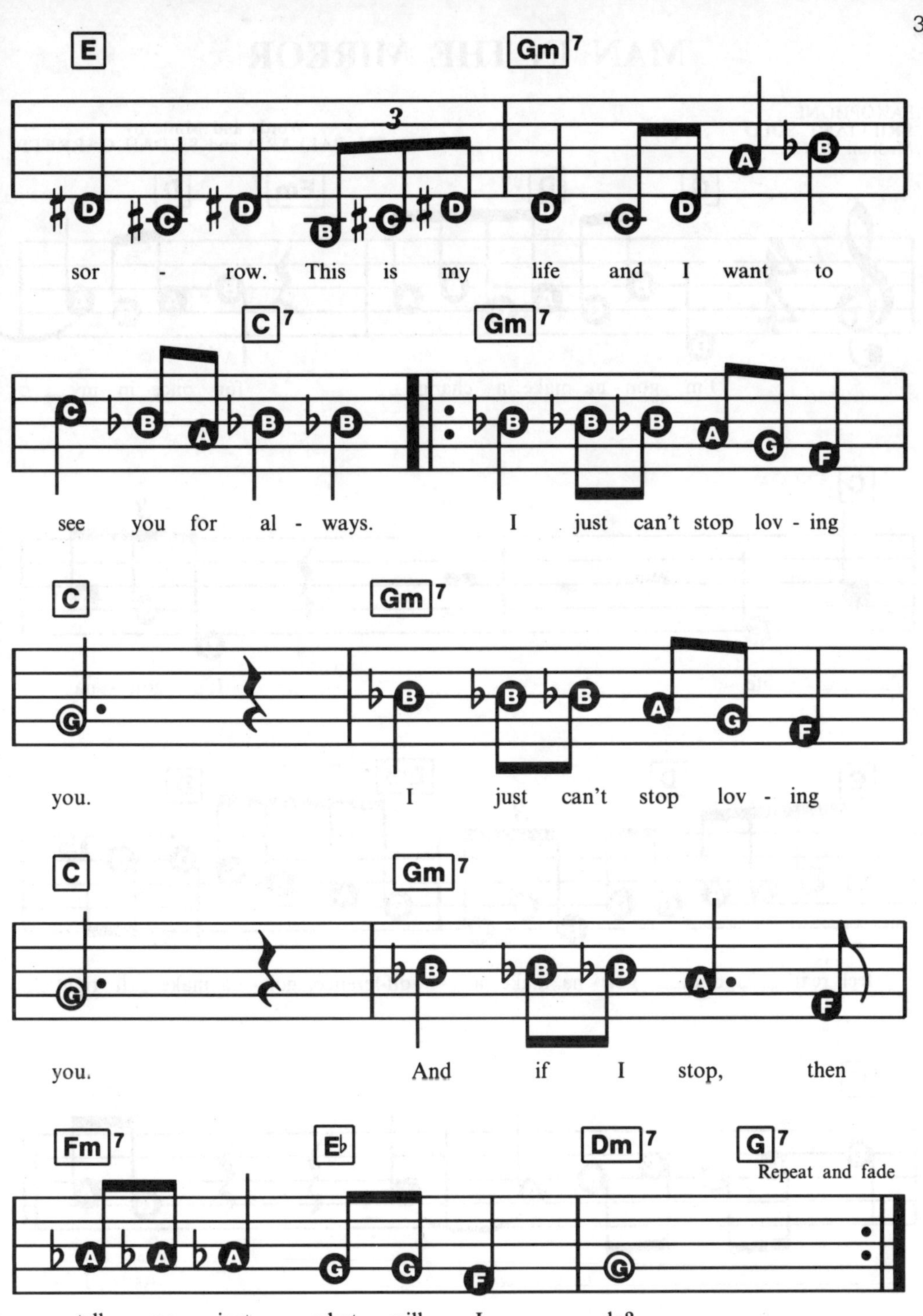
E
Gm7
sor - row. This is my life and I want to
C7
Gm7
see you for al - ways. I just can't stop lov - ing
C
Gm7
you. I just can't stop lov - ing
C
Gm7
you. And if I stop, then
Fm7
E♭
Dm7
G7
Repeat and fade
tell me just what will I do?

MAN IN THE MIRROR

SAXOPHONE
BRILLIANT SOLO
Medium ROCK

Words and Music by
GLEN BALLARD and SIEDAH GARRETT

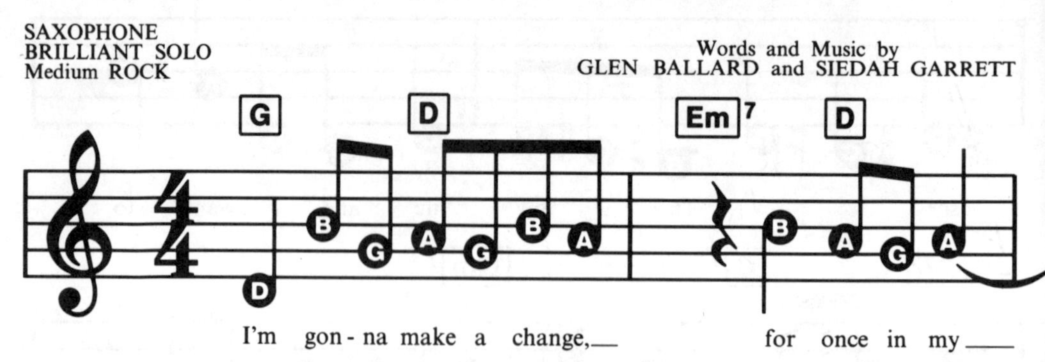

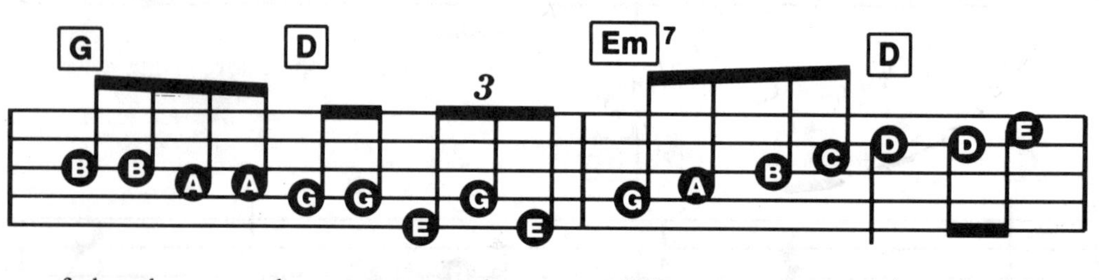

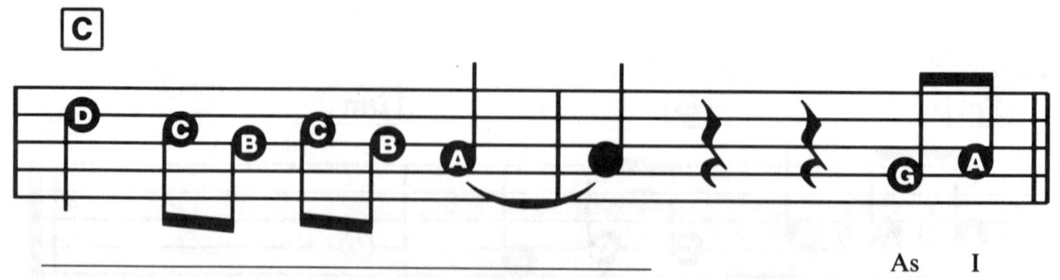

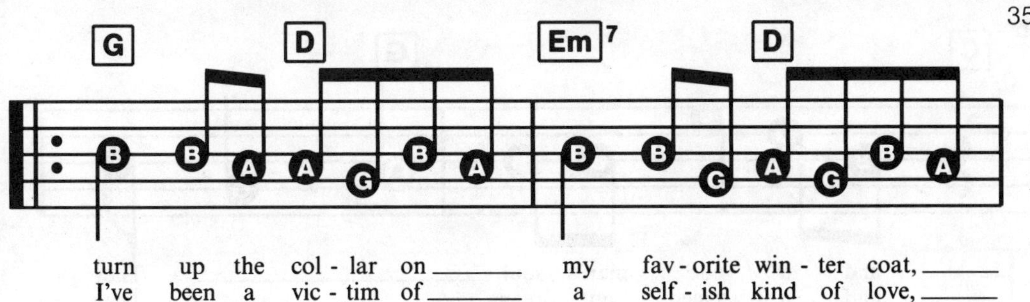
G D Em7 D
turn up the col - lar on ___ my fav - orite win - ter coat, ___
I've been a vic - tim of ___ a self - ish kind of love, ___

C
3
this wind is blow - in' my mind. I see the
It's time I re - a - lize, that there are

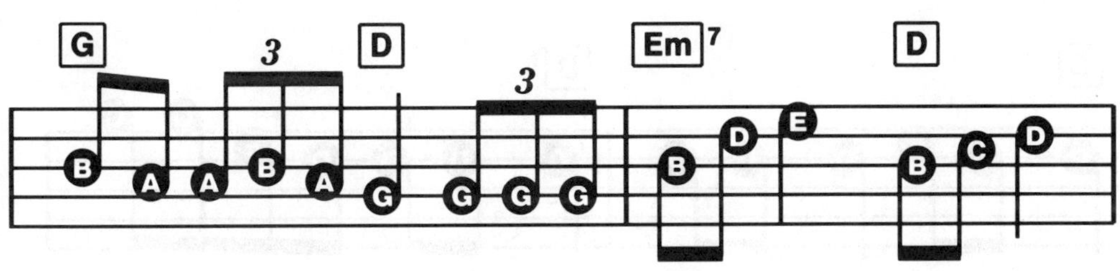
G D Em7 D
3 3
kids ___ in the street ___ with not e - nough to eat. Who am I
some with no home, ___ not a nick - el to loan. Could it be

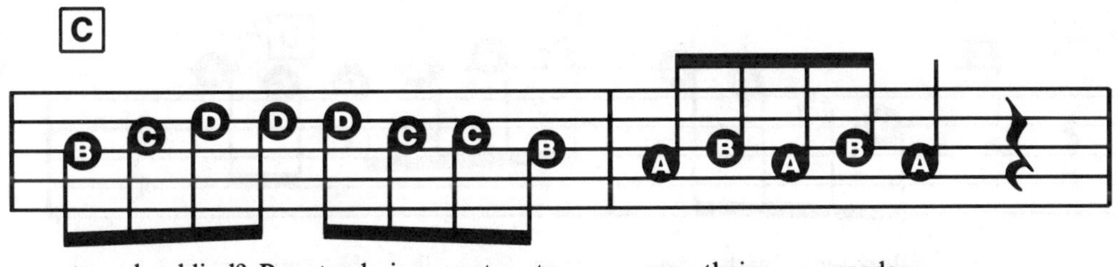
C D
to be blind? Pre - tend - ing not to see their ___ needs. ___
real - ly me, pre - tend - ing that they're not a - lone? ___

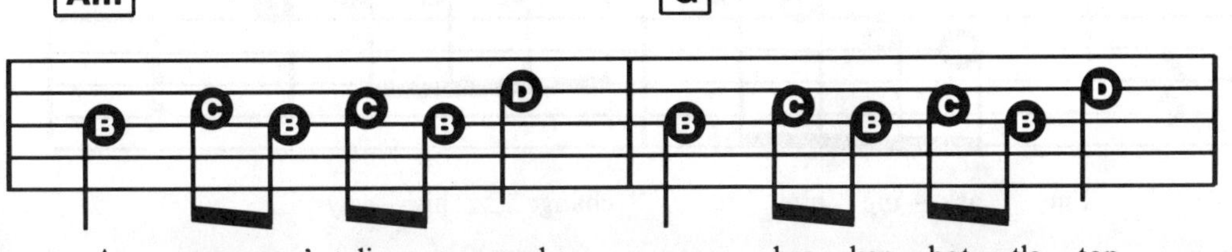
Am7 G
A sum - mer's dis - re - gard, a bro - ken bot - tle top,
A wil - low deep - ly scarred, some - bod - y's brok - en heart,

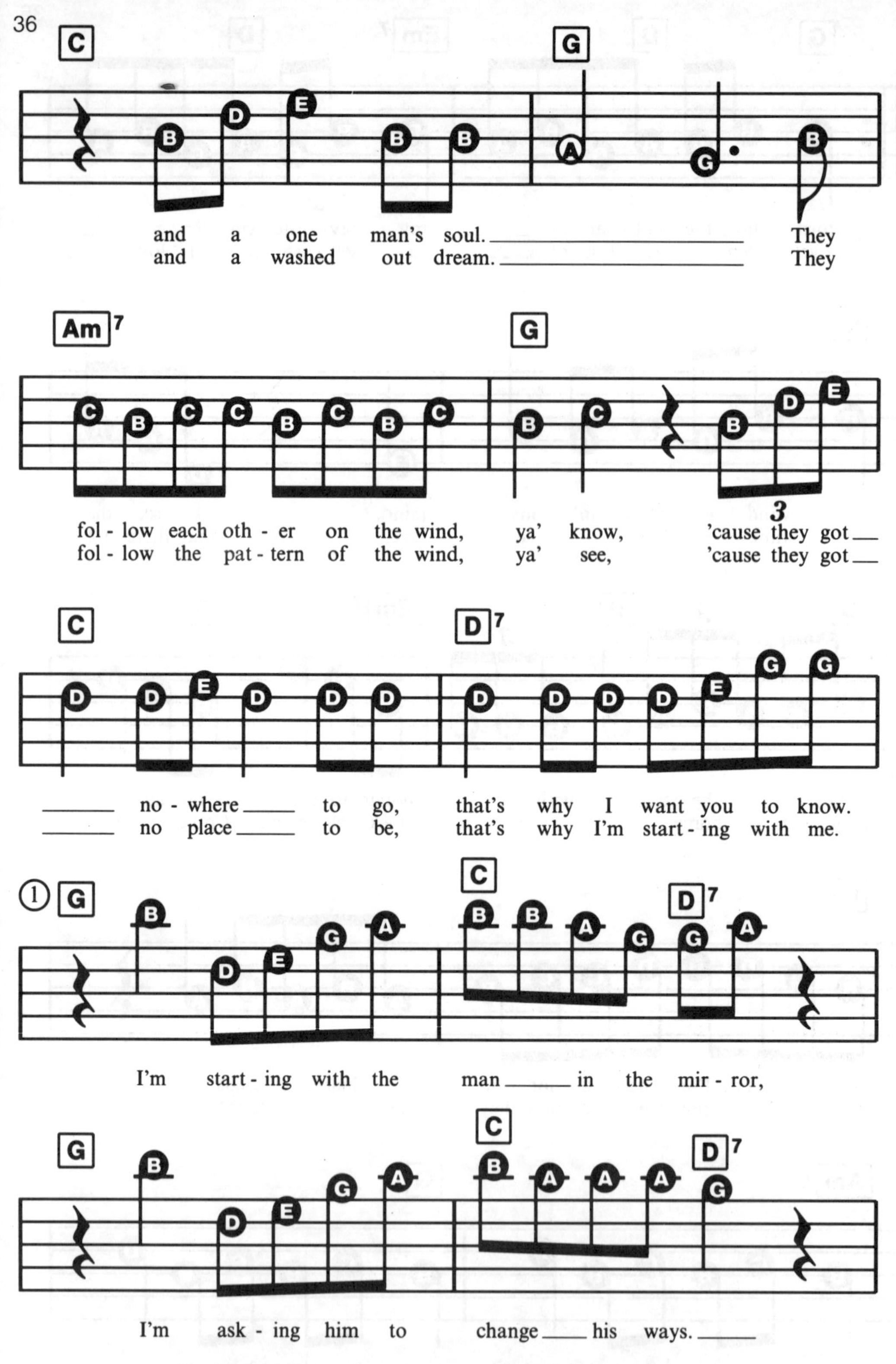
C
G
and a one man's soul. They
and a washed out dream. They
Am7
G
fol - low each oth - er on the wind, ya' know, 'cause they got
fol - low the pat - tern of the wind, ya' see, 'cause they got
3
C
D7
no - where to go, that's why I want you to know.
no place to be, that's why I'm start - ing with me.
1
G
C
D7
I'm start - ing with the man in the mir - ror,
G
C
D7
I'm ask - ing him to change his ways.

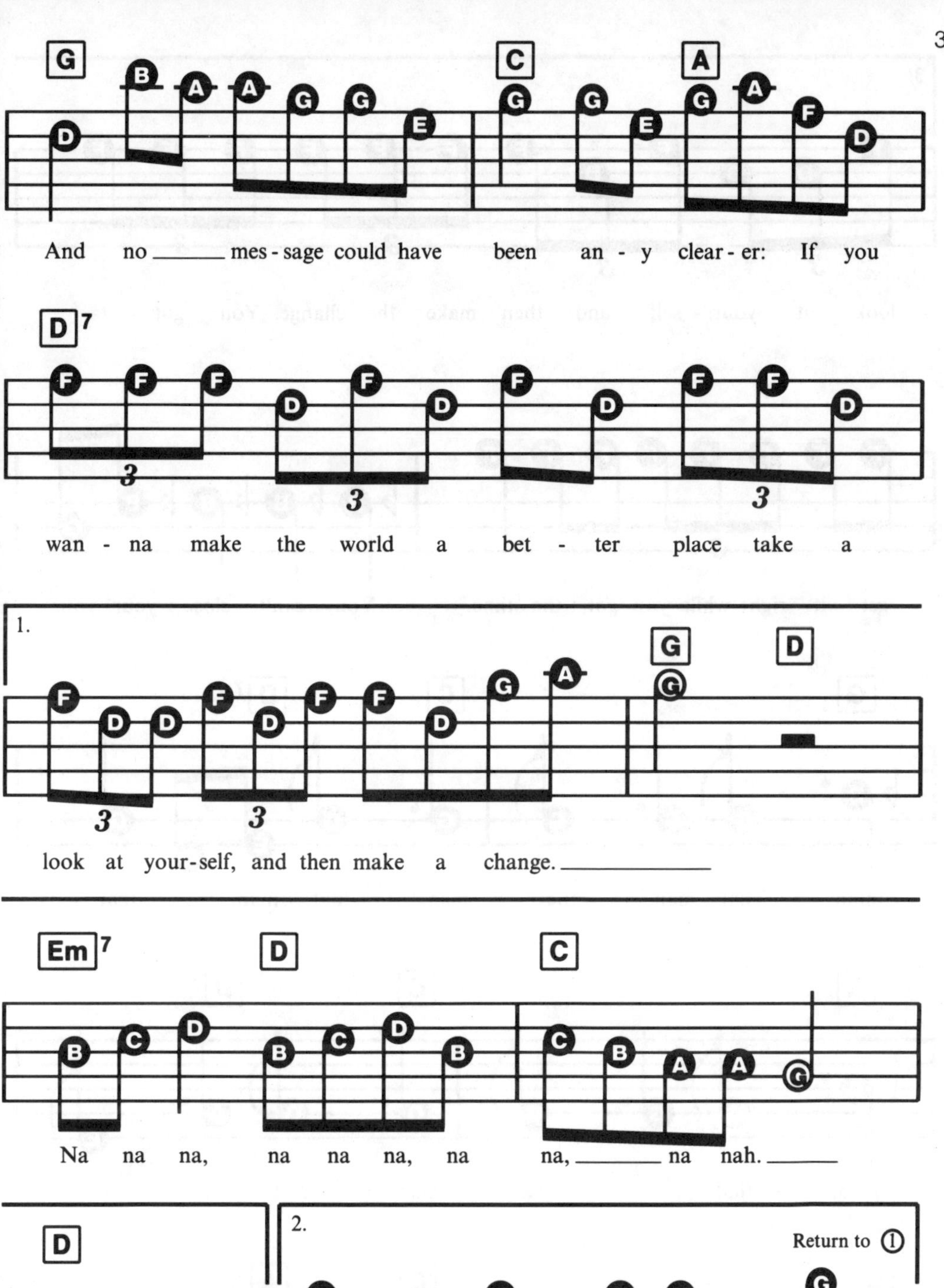
G C A
D B A A G G E G G E G A F D
And no ___ mes-sage could have been an-y clear-er: If you
D7
F F F D F D F D F F D
3 3 3
wan-na make the world a bet-ter place take a
1.
G D
F D D F D F F D G A G
3 3
look at your-self, and then make a change. ___
Em7 D C
B C D B C D B C B A A G
Na na na, na na na, na na, ___ na nah. ___
D
2.
Return to ①
F D D F D F F D G
3 3
look at your-self and then make that change.

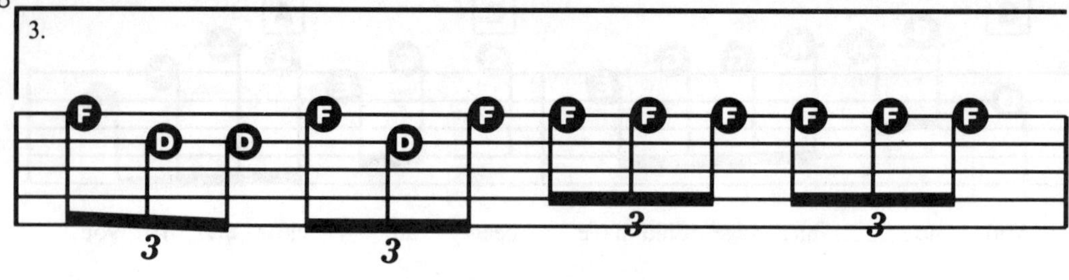
3.
F
D
D
F
D
F
F
F
F
F
F
F
3
3
3
3
look at your - self and then make the change. You got - ta

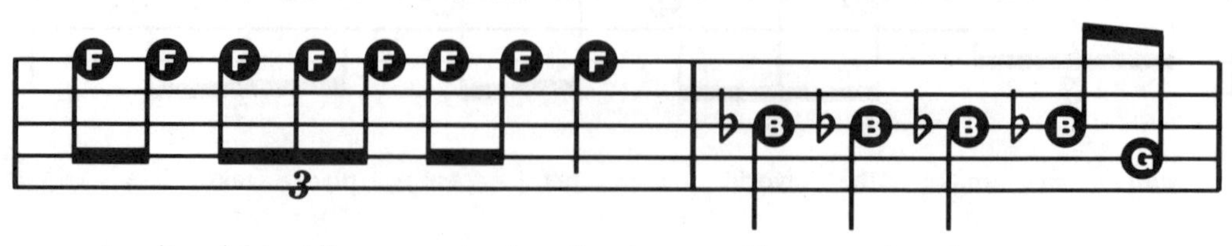
F
F
F
F
F
F
F
F
3
B
B
B
B
G
get it right while you got the time. You can't close your, your

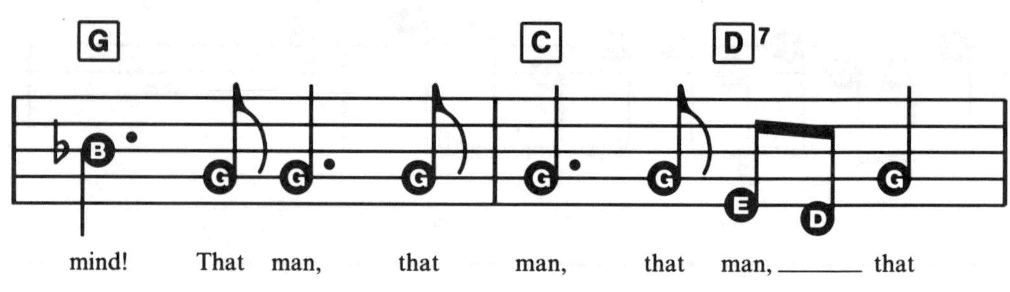
G
C
D7
B
G
G
G
G
G
E
D
G
mind! That man, that man, that man, that

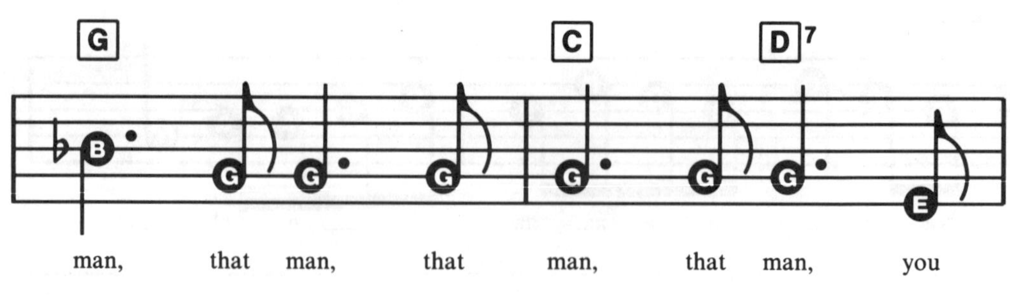
G
C
D7
B
G
G
G
G
G
G
E
man, that man, that man, that man, you

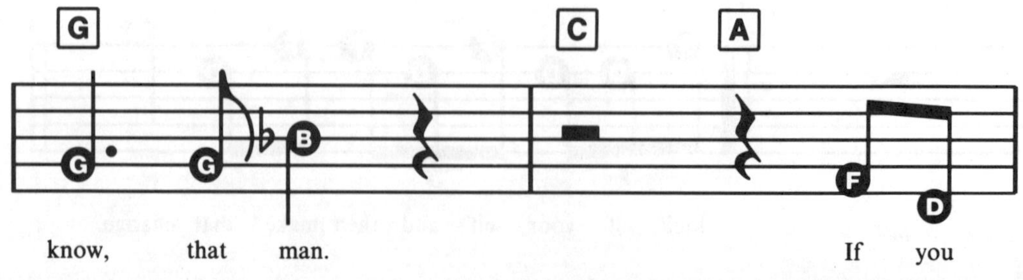
G
C
A
G
G
B
F
D
know, that man. If you

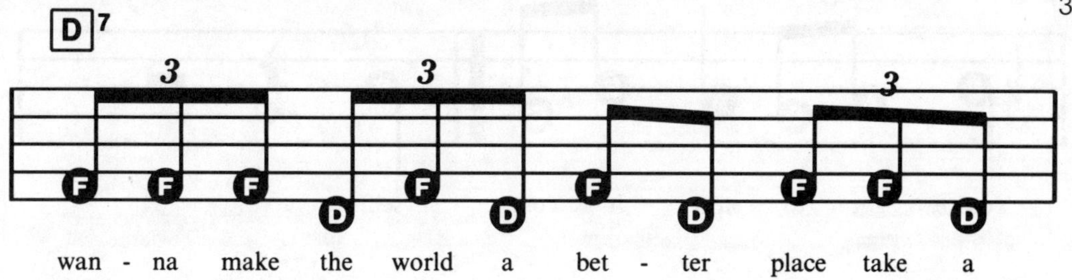
D7
3
3
3
F F F D F D F D F F D
wan - na make the world a bet - ter place take a

3
3
G
D
F F D F D F F D G G
look at your-self and then make a change. Hoo!

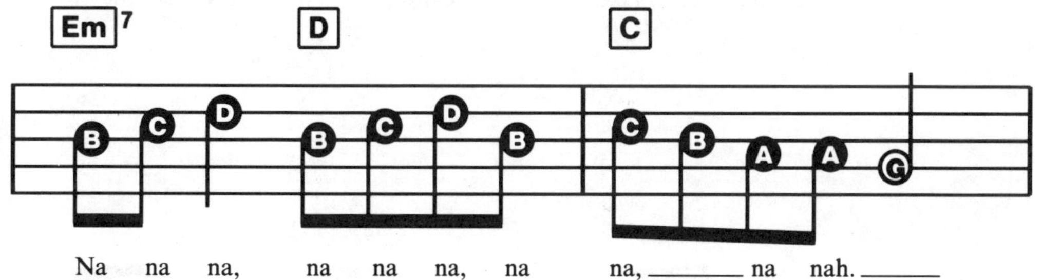
Em7
D
C
B C D B C D B C B A A G
Na na na, na na na, na na, na nah.

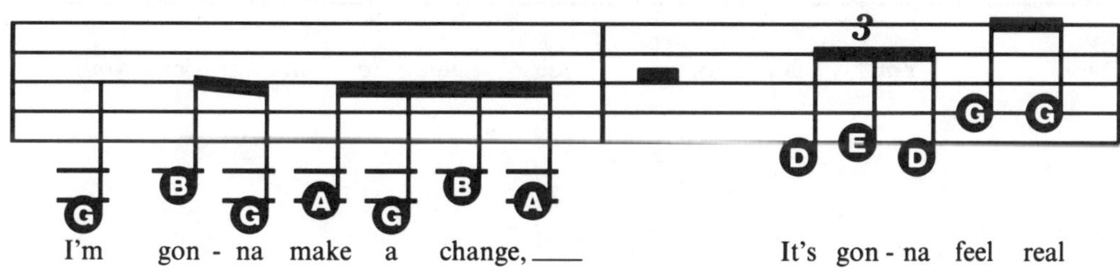
3
G B G A G B A D E D G G
I'm gon - na make a change, It's gon - na feel real

B G E E G G B G A
good! Come on! Just lift your - self, you know.

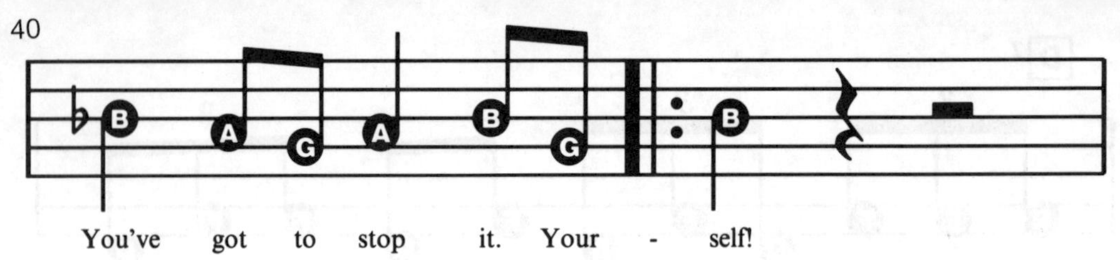
B A G A B G B
You've got to stop it. Your - self!

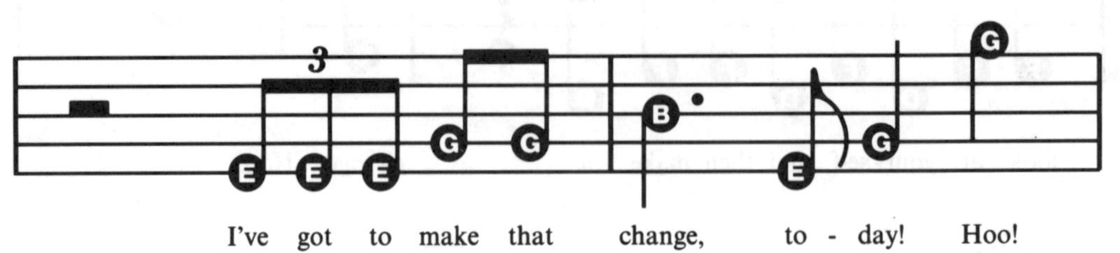
3
E E E G G B E G G
I've got to make that change, to - day! Hoo!

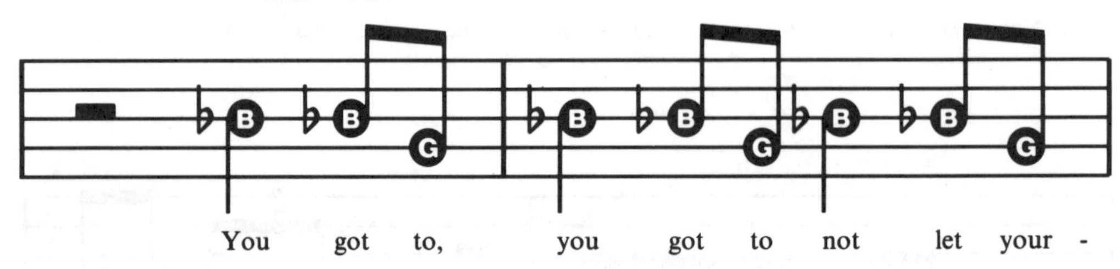
B B G B B G B B G
You got to, you got to not let your -

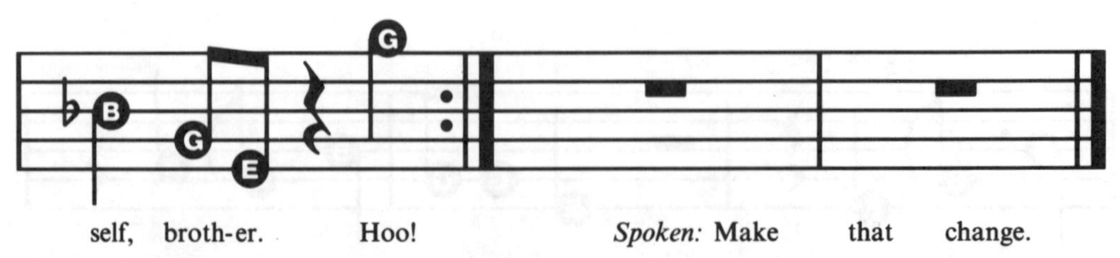
B G E G
self, broth-er. Hoo!
Spoken: Make that change.

MUSCLES

TROMBONE
BRIGHT 'N' BRASSY
Fast ROCK or DISCO
Words and Music by
MICHAEL JACKSON
N.C.
G
She said she wants a man ___ to
say they have to see ___ his
Dm7 Gm7 C B♭
al - ways un - der - stand. ___ But that's all right for her.
real person - al - i - ty. ___ But that's all right for them.
A C
Still it ain't e - nough for me. ___ She
Still it ain't e - nough for me. ___ But I
1
Dm G Dm7
said she wants a guy ___ to keep her sat - is -
need what the eyes can see: ___ ah, his an - at - o -
said she wants a man ___ to al - ways un - der -

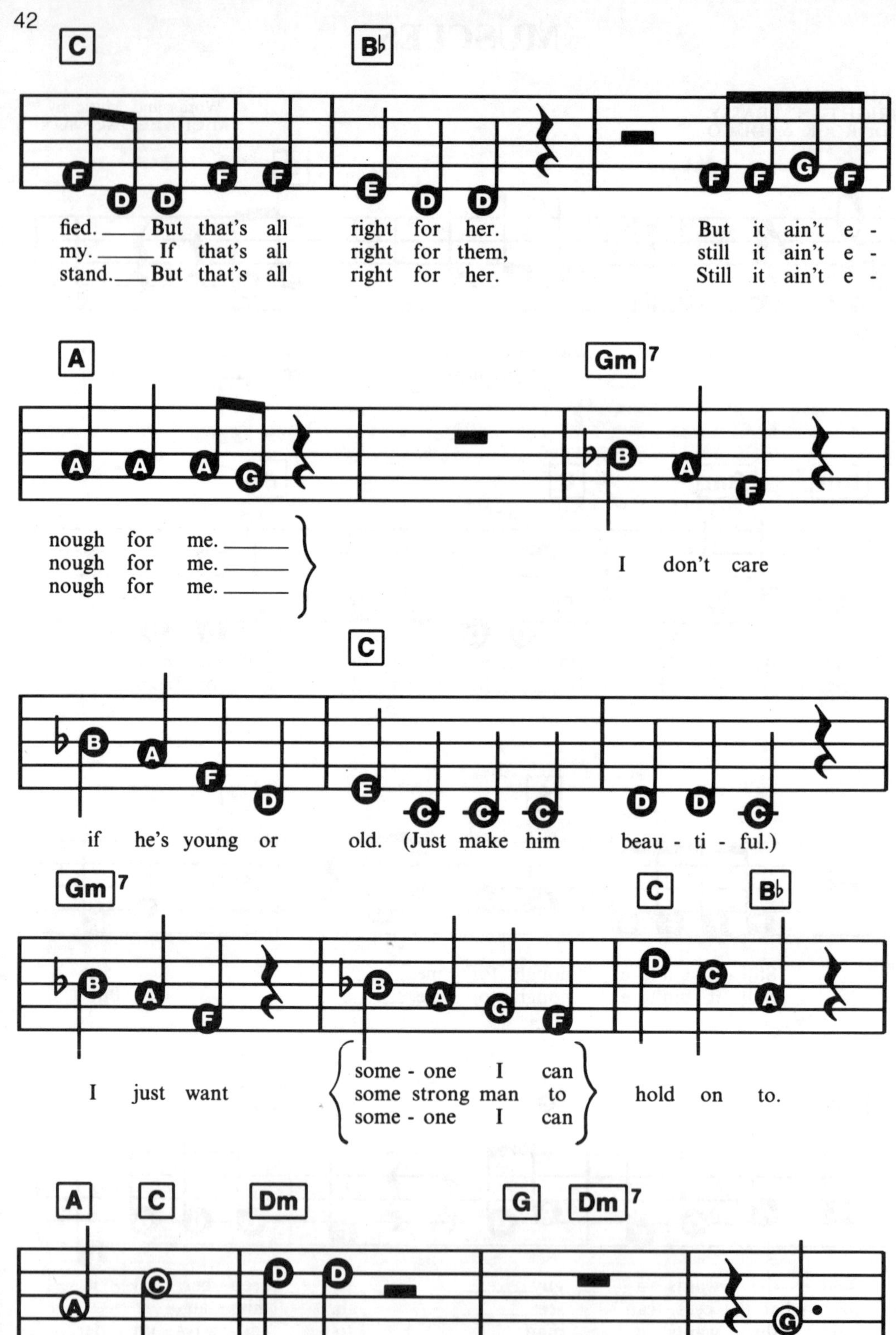
C
B♭
F D D F F
E D D
F F G F
fied. ___ But that's all right for her. But it ain't e -
my. ___ If that's all right for them, still it ain't e -
stand. ___ But that's all right for her. Still it ain't e -
A
Gm7
A A A G
B A F
nough for me. ___
nough for me. ___
nough for me. ___
I don't care
C
B A F D
E C C C
D D C
if he's young or old. (Just make him beau - ti - ful.)
Gm7
C
B♭
B A F
B A G F
D C A
I just want
some - one I can
some strong man to
some - one I can
hold on to.
A
C
Dm
G
Dm7
A C
D D
G
I want mus - cles,
all,

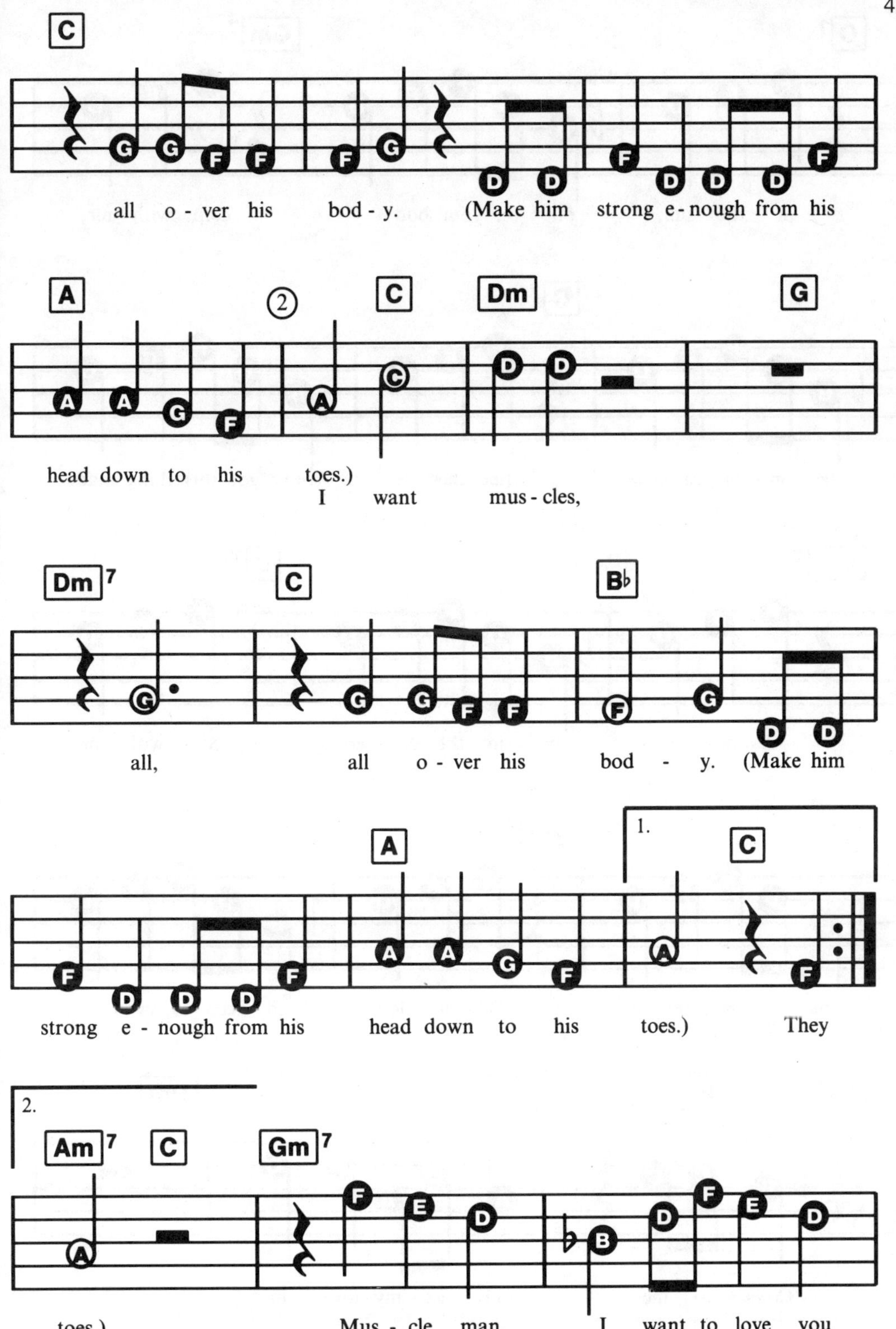
C
G G F F F G D D F D D D F
all o - ver his bod - y. (Make him strong e - nough from his
A ② C Dm G
A A G F A C D D
head down to his toes.)
I want mus - cles,
Dm7 C B♭
G G G F F F G D D
all, all o - ver his bod - y. (Make him
A 1. C
F D D D F A A G F A F
strong e - nough from his head down to his toes.) They
2.
Am7 C Gm7
A F E D B D F E D
toes.) Mus - cle man, I want to love you

C7
Gm7
F E D
B D F E D
F E D
in the sun; oil on your bod - y come with me;

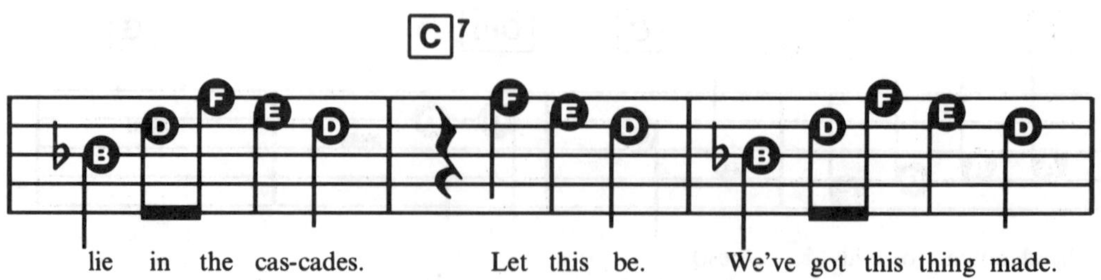
C7
B D F E D
F E D
B D F E D
lie in the cas-cades. Let this be. We've got this thing made.

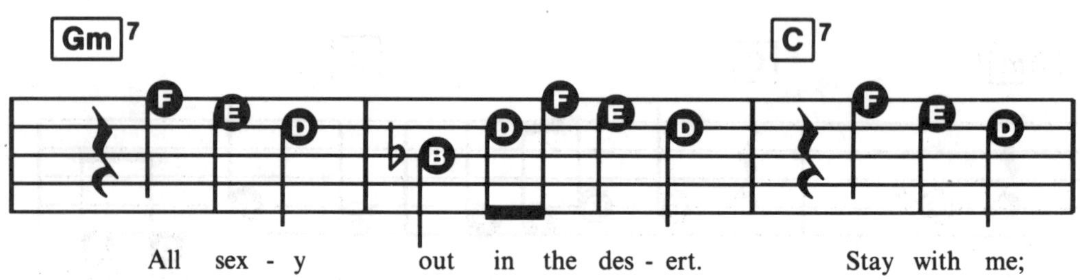
Gm7
C7
F E D
B D F E D
F E D
All sex - y out in the des - ert. Stay with me;

Gm7
B D F E D
F E D
B D F E D
you won't re - gret it. Take this love, so deep to swim in,

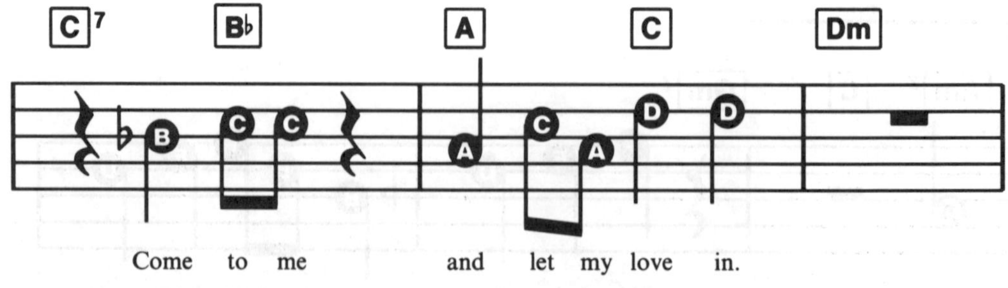
C7
B♭
A
C
Dm
B C C
A C A D D
Come to me and let my love in.

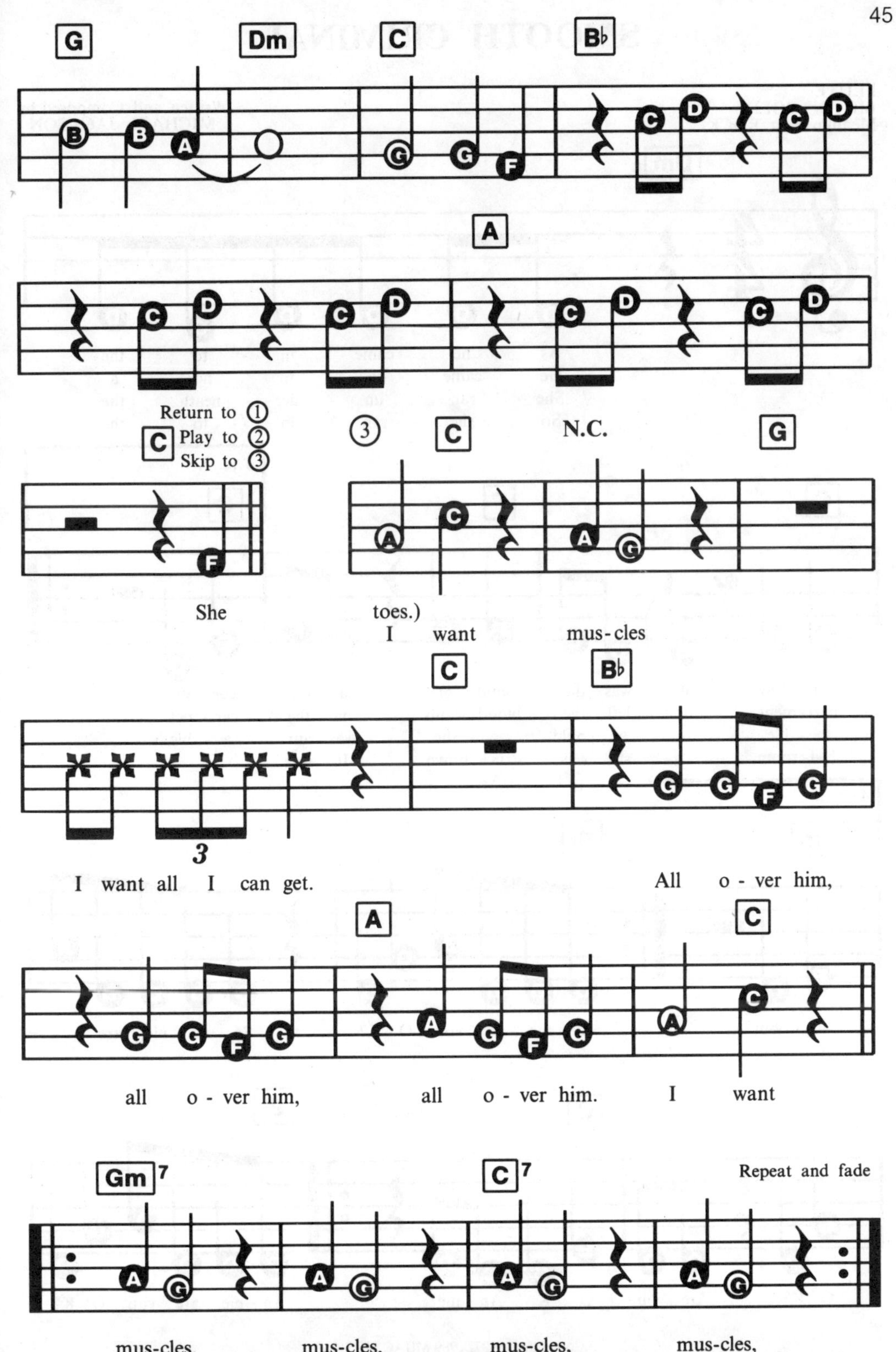
G
Dm
C
B♭
A
Return to ①
C
Play to ②
Skip to ③
③
C
N.C.
G
She
toes.)
I want mus-cles
C
B♭
3
I want all I can get.
All o - ver him,
A
C
all o - ver him,
all o - ver him.
I want
Gm7
C7
Repeat and fade
mus-cles,
mus-cles,
mus-cles,
mus-cles,

SMOOTH CRIMINAL

A
A A A A A C A B A
So An - nie, are you O K? Are you
Dm C
C A C D F F F F E C D E
O K, An - nie? (An - nie, are you O K?) (Will you
B♭ C Dm
D B D D C A F F F F F
tell us that you're O K?) (There's a sign in the
C B♭ A
E C F G D B D D C C E F
win - dow) (that he struck you - a cre - scen - do, An - nie.)
Dm C
F F F F F F E C D D E
(He came in - to your a - part - ment.) (He left the

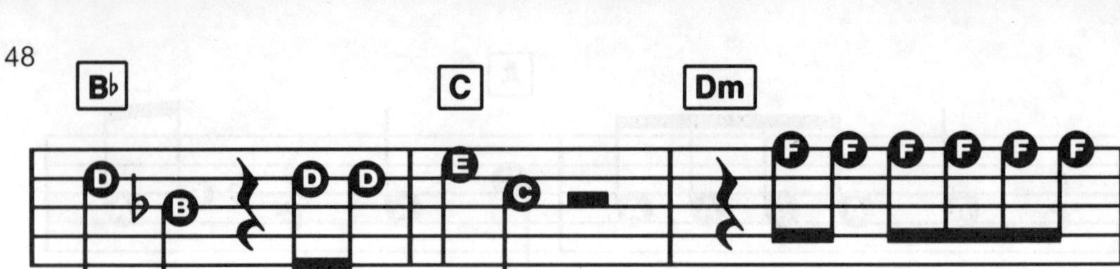
B♭
C
Dm
D B D D E C F F F F F F
blood - stains on the car - pet.) (Then you ran in - to the

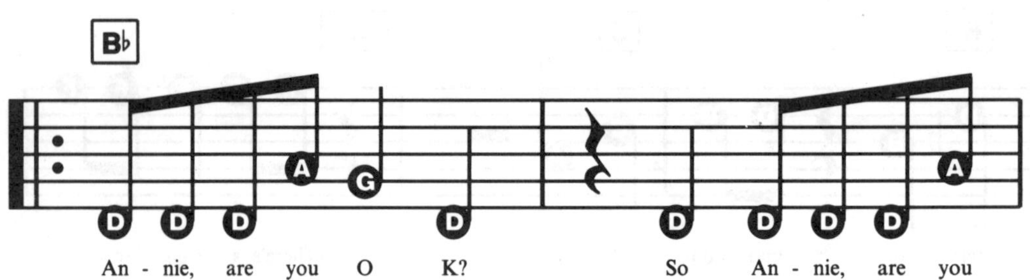
C
B♭
A
E C D E D B D D E C
bed - room,) (you were struck down.) (It was your doom.)

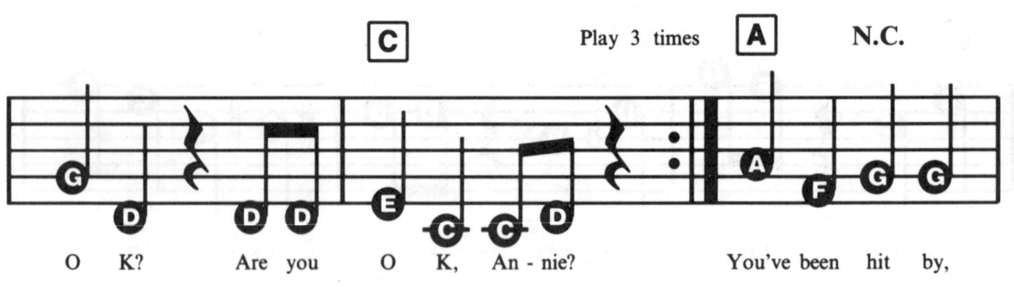
B♭
D D D A G D D D D D A
An - nie, are you O K? So An - nie, are you

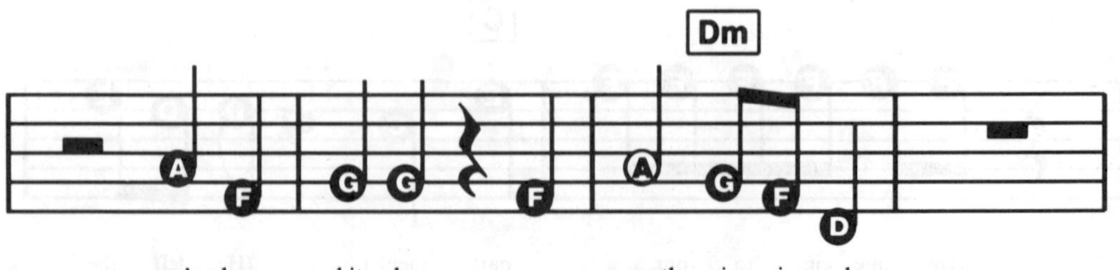
C
Play 3 times
A
N.C.
G D D D E C C D A F G G
O K? Are you O K, An - nie? You've been hit by,
Dm
A F G G F A G F D
you've been hit by - a smooth crim - i - nal.

C

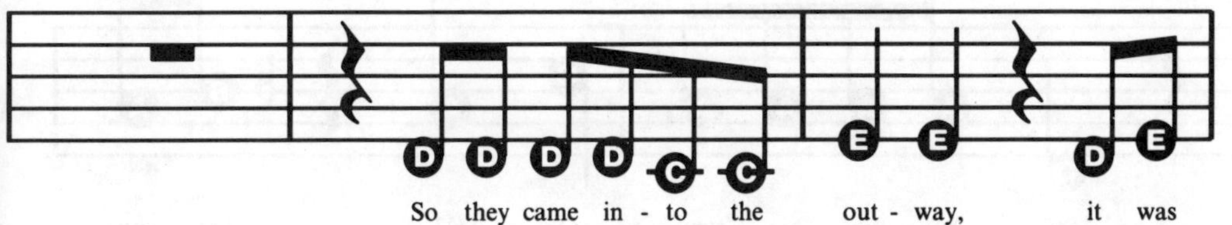
So they came in - to the out - way, it was

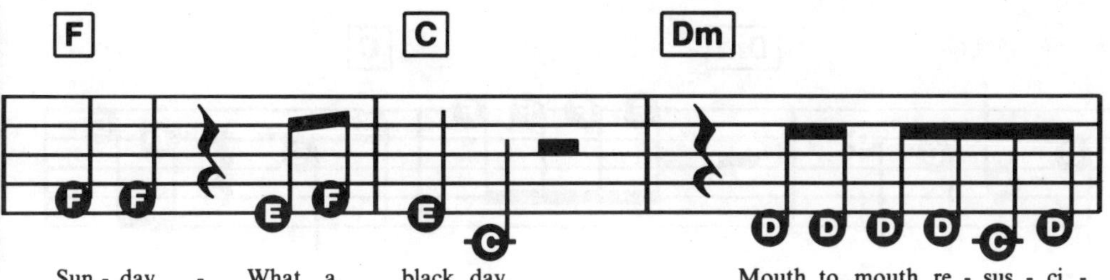
F
C
Dm
Sun - day - What a black day. Mouth to mouth re - sus - ci -

C
F
C
ta - tion, sound- ing heart - beats - in - tim - i - da - tions.

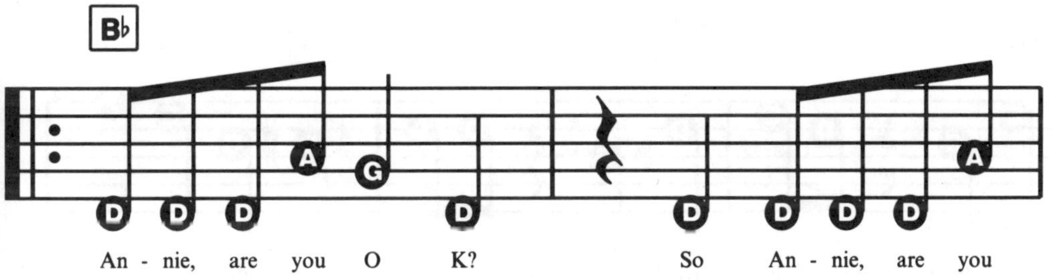
B♭
An - nie, are you O K? So An - nie, are you

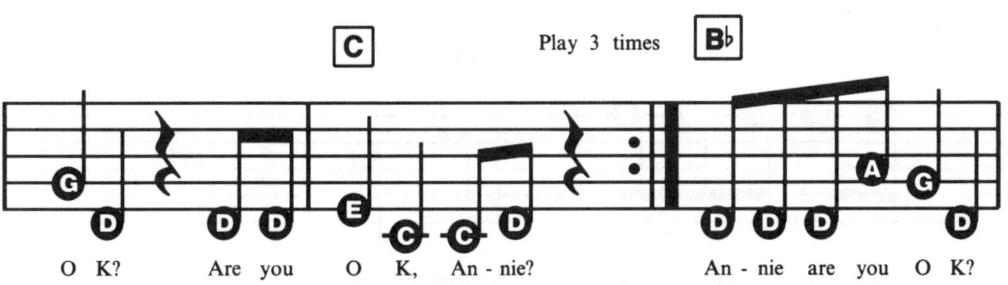
C
Play 3 times
B♭
O K? Are you O K, An - nie? An - nie are you O K?

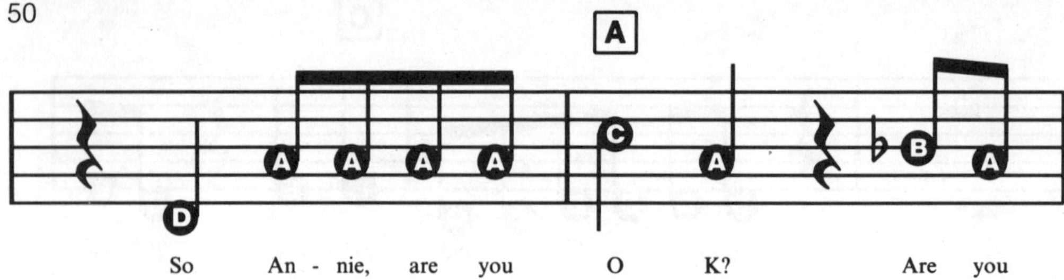
A
So An - nie, are you O K? Are you

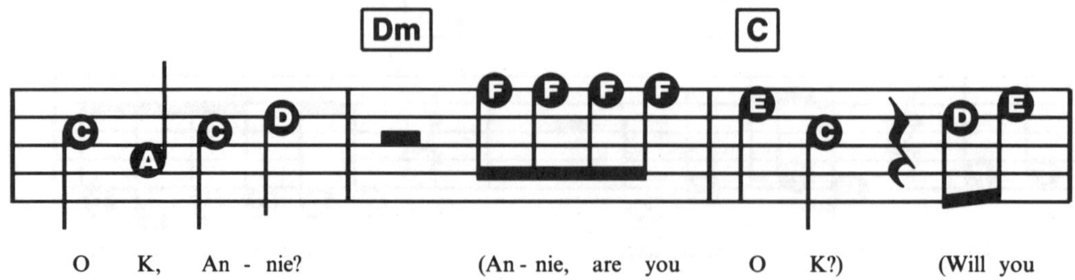
Dm
C
O K, An - nie? (An - nie, are you O K?) (Will you

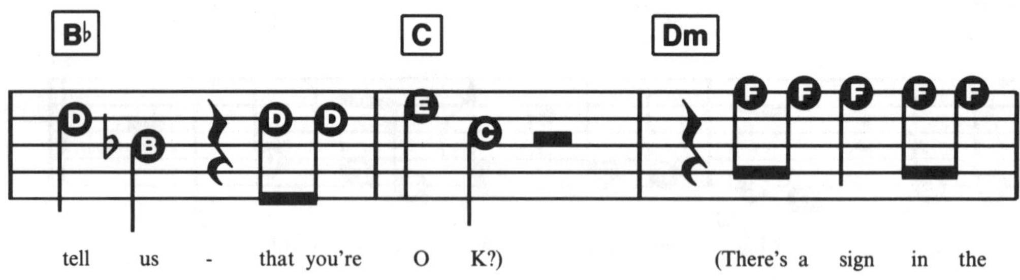
B♭
C
Dm
tell us - that you're O K?) (There's a sign in the

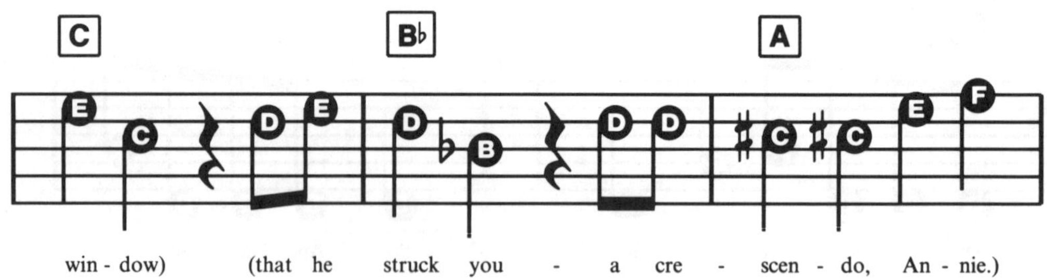
C
B♭
A
win - dow) (that he struck you - a cre - scen - do, An - nie.)

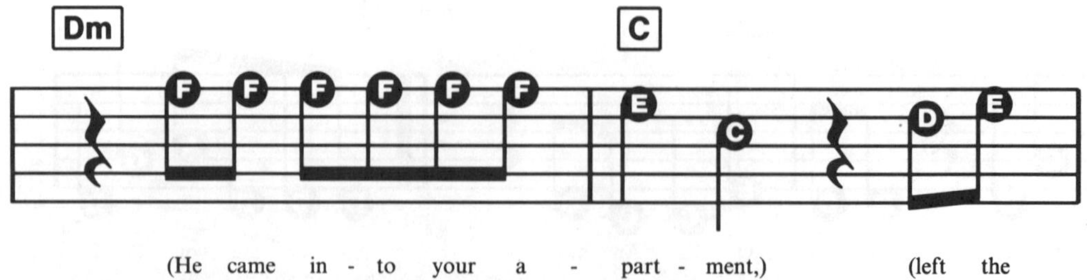
Dm
C
(He came in - to your a - part - ment,) (left the

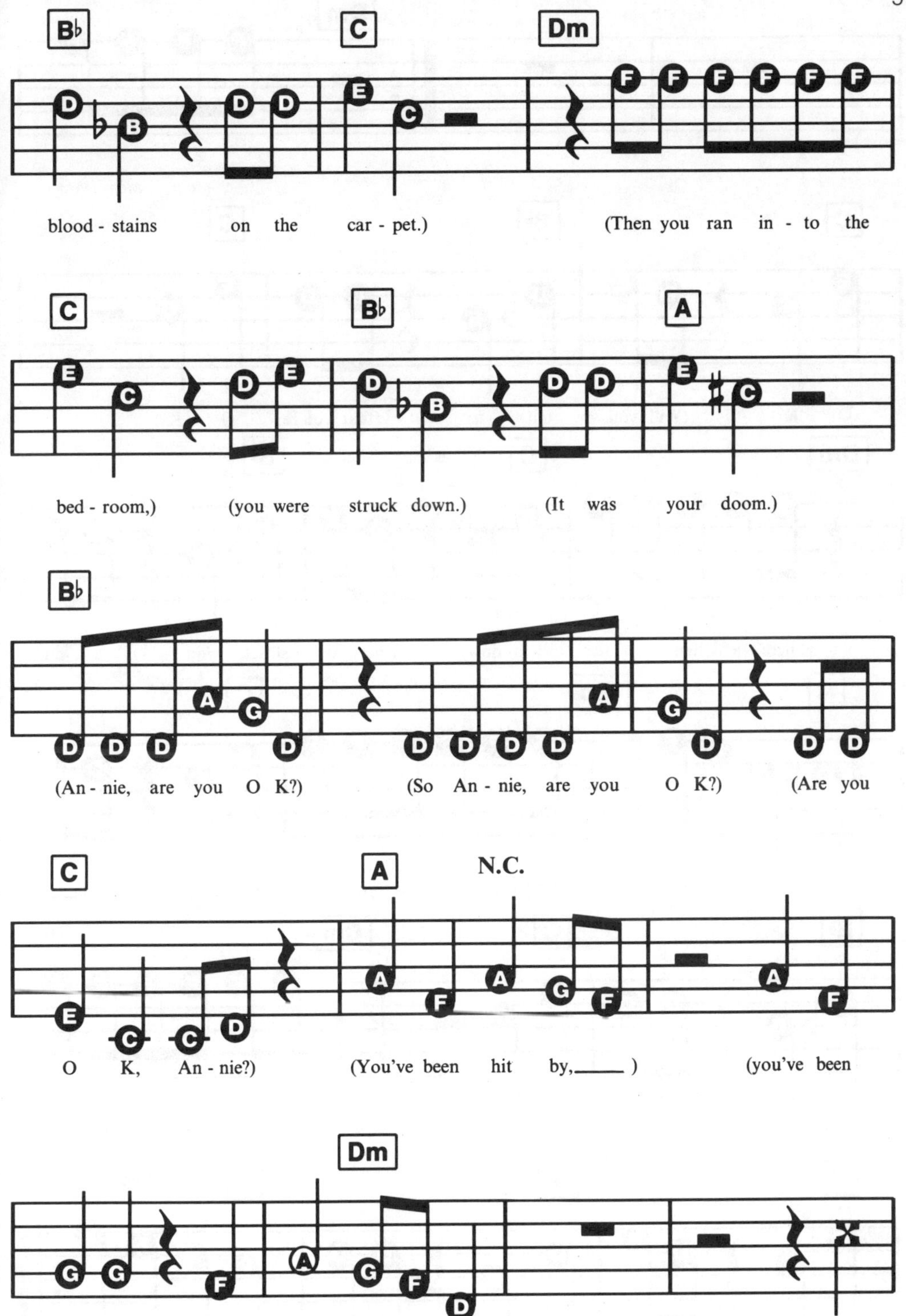
B♭
C
Dm
blood - stains on the car - pet.) (Then you ran in - to the
C
B♭
A
bed - room,) (you were struck down.) (It was your doom.)
B♭
(An - nie, are you O K?) (So An - nie, are you O K?) (Are you
C
A
N.C.
O K, An - nie?) (You've been hit by, ____) (you've been
Dm
struck by - a smooth crim - i - nal.)
(Spoken:) Okay, I want everybody to clear the area right now!
Aaow!

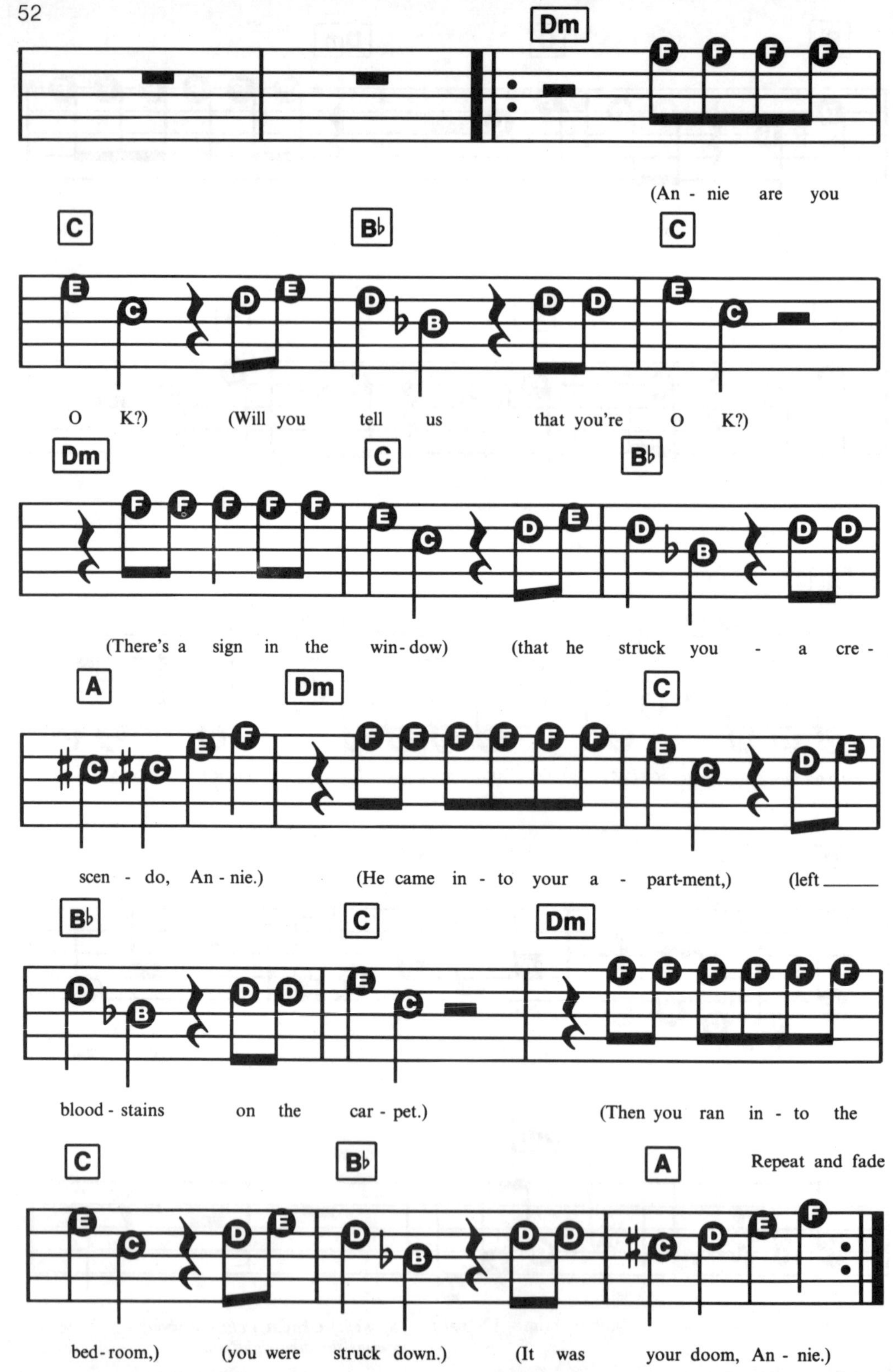
Dm
(An - nie are you
C Bb C
O K?) (Will you tell us that you're O K?)
Dm C Bb
(There's a sign in the win - dow) (that he struck you - a cre -
A Dm C
scen - do, An - nie.) (He came in - to your a - part-ment,) (left
Bb C Dm
blood - stains on the car - pet.) (Then you ran in - to the
C Bb A
Repeat and fade
bed - room,) (you were struck down.) (It was your doom, An - nie.)

THE WAY YOU MAKE ME FEEL

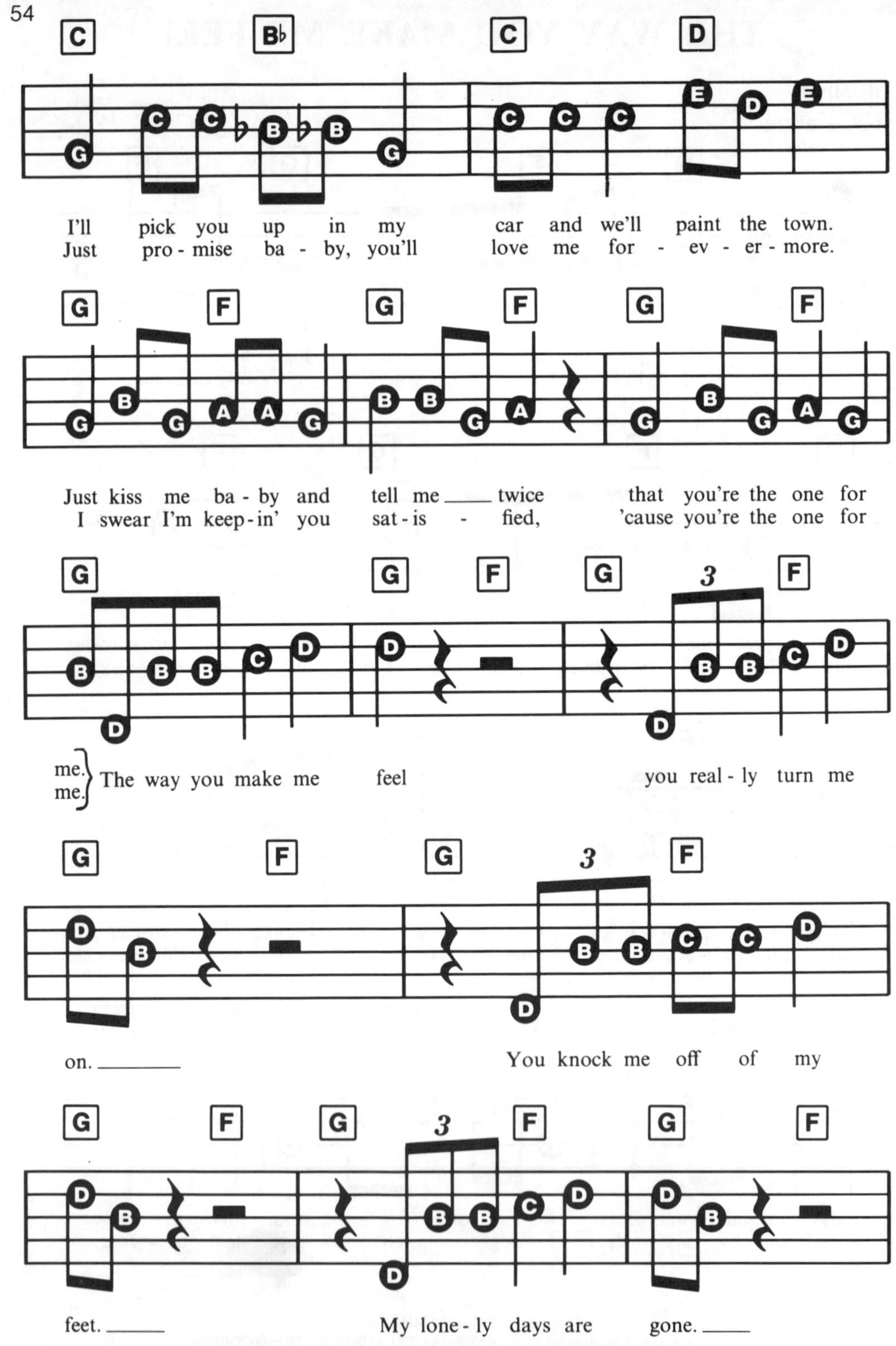
C Bb C D
I'll pick you up in my car and we'll paint the town.
Just pro - mise ba - by, you'll love me for - ev - er - more.
G F G F G F
Just kiss me ba - by and tell me ___ twice that you're the one for
I swear I'm keep - in' you sat - is - fied, 'cause you're the one for
G G F G 3 F
me.
me.
The way you make me feel you real - ly turn me
G F G 3 F
on. ___ You knock me off of my
G F G 3 F G F
feet. ___ My lone - ly days are gone. ___

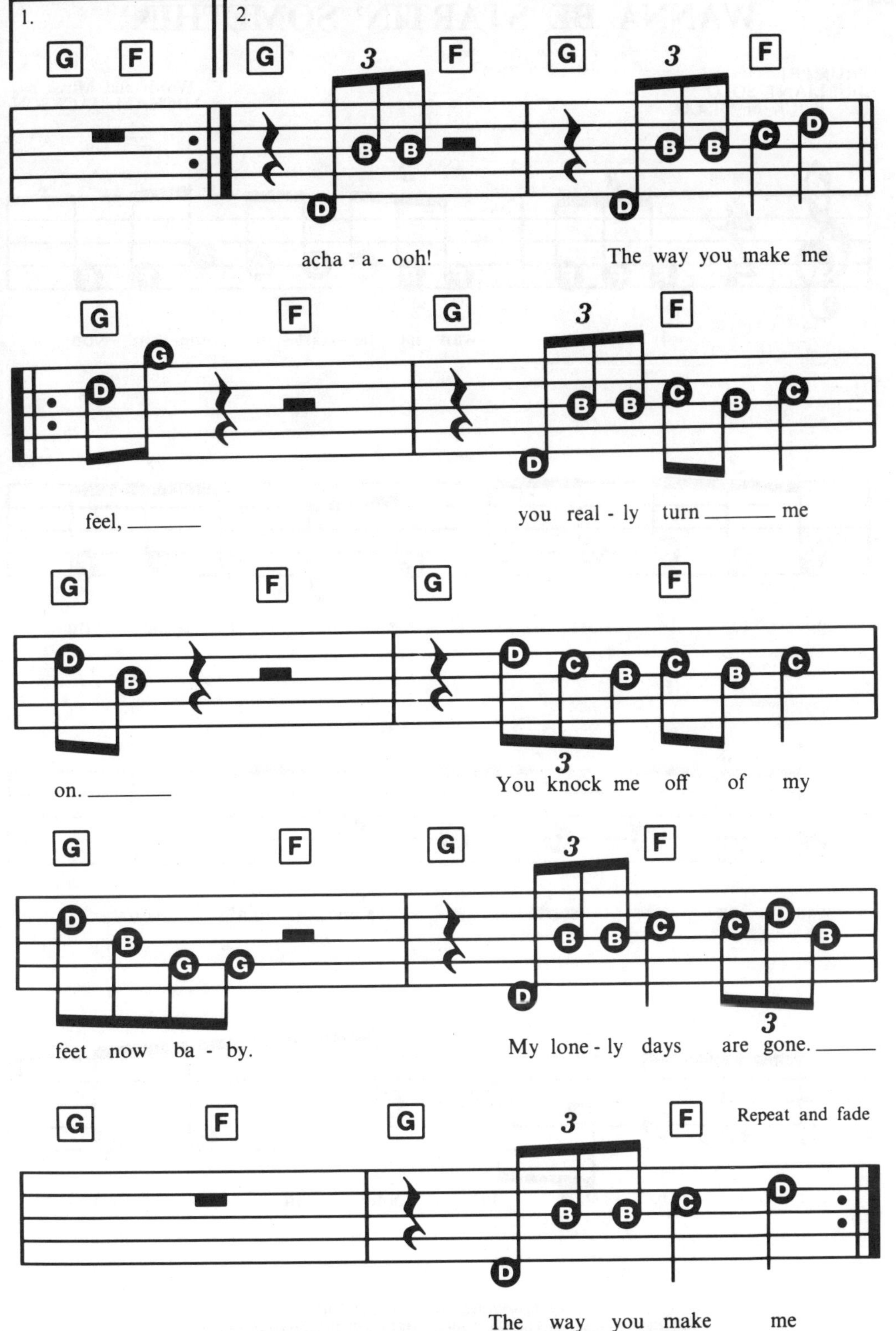
1.
2.
G F G F G F
acha - a - ooh! The way you make me
feel, you real - ly turn me
on. You knock me off of my
feet now ba - by. My lone - ly days are gone.
Repeat and fade
The way you make me

WANNA BE STARTIN' SOMETHIN'

TRUMPET
BRILLIANT SOLO
Fast ROCK or DISCO

Words and Music by
MICHAEL JACKSON

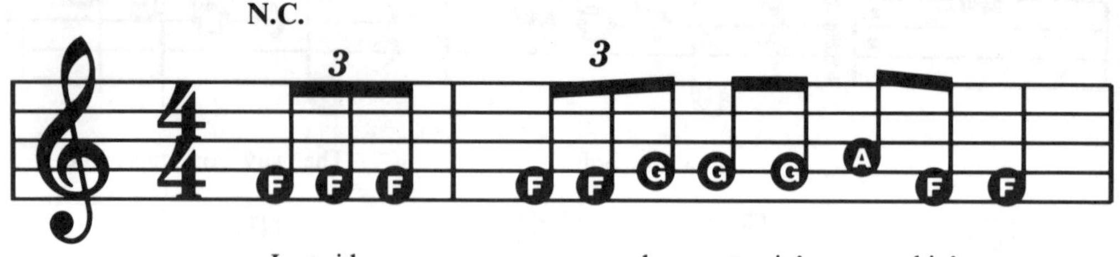

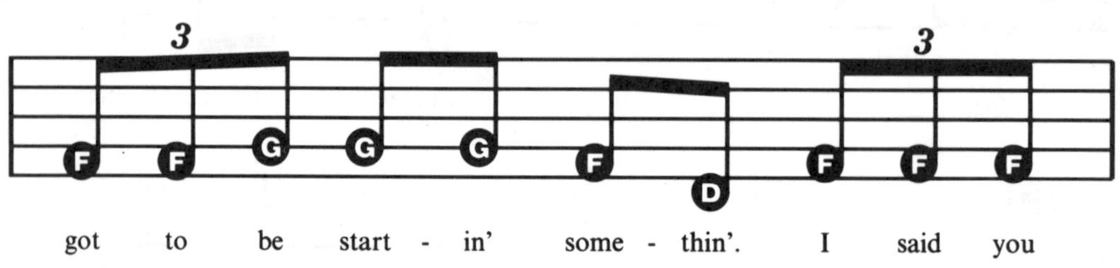

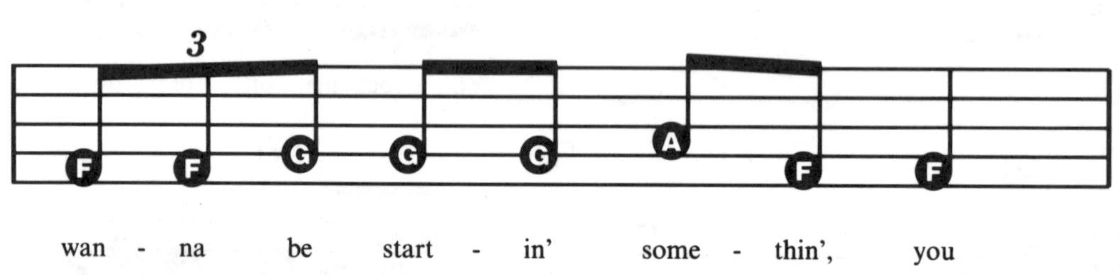

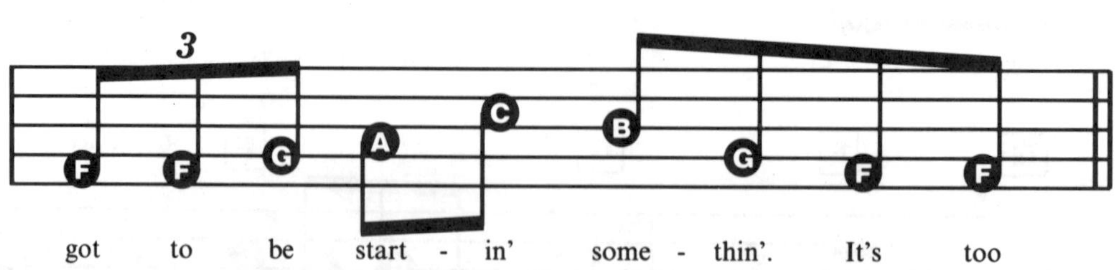

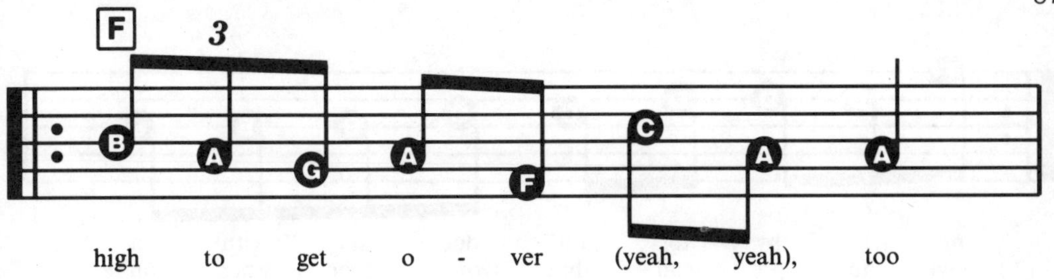
F
3
B A G A F C A A
high to get o - ver (yeah, yeah), too

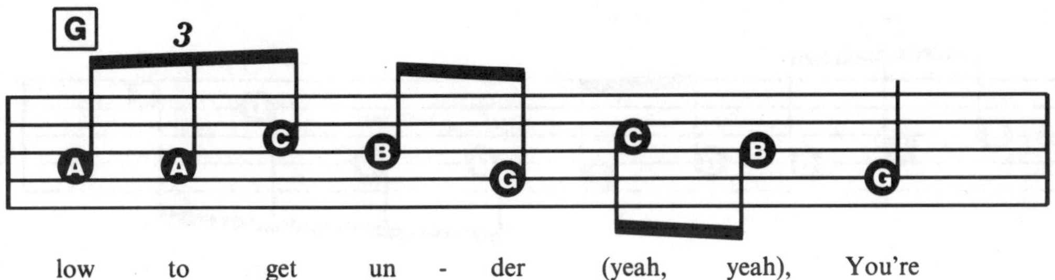
G
3
A A C B G C B G
low to get un - der (yeah, yeah), You're

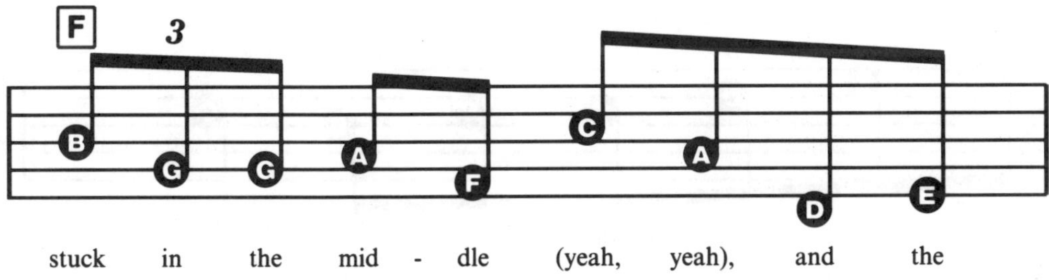
F
3
B G G A F C A D E
stuck in the mid - dle (yeah, yeah), and the

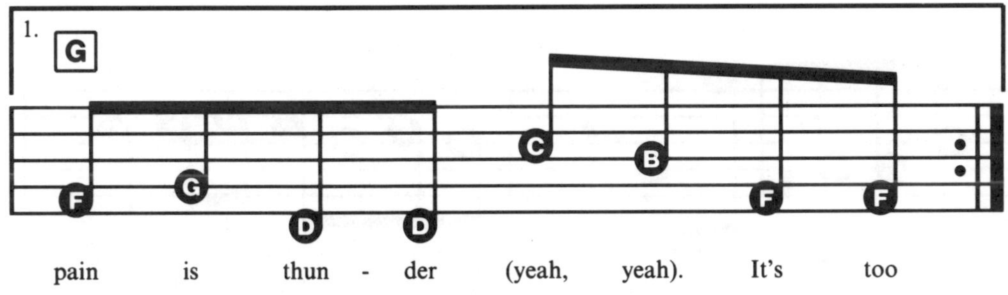
1.
G
F G D D C B F F
pain is thun - der (yeah, yeah). It's too

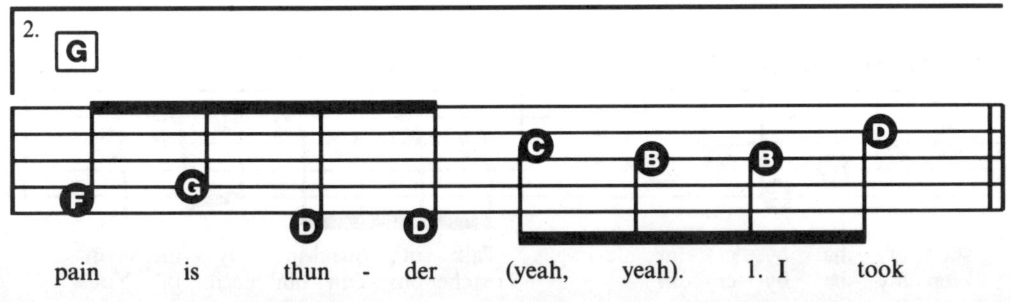
2.
G
F G D D C B B D
pain is thun - der (yeah, yeah). 1. I took

N.C.

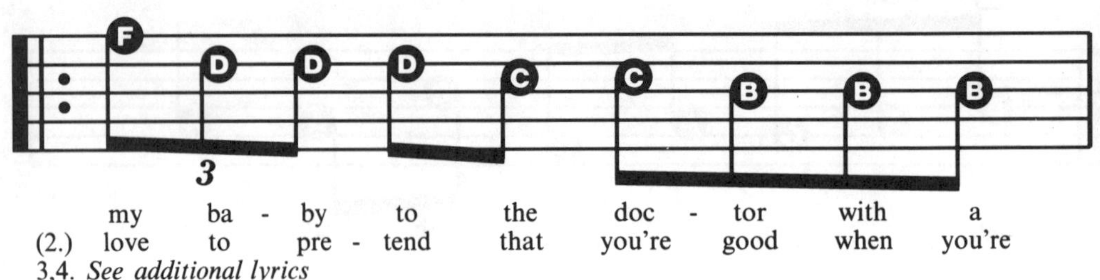
3
my ba - by to the doc - tor with a
(2.) love to pre - tend that you're good when you're
3,4. See additional lyrics

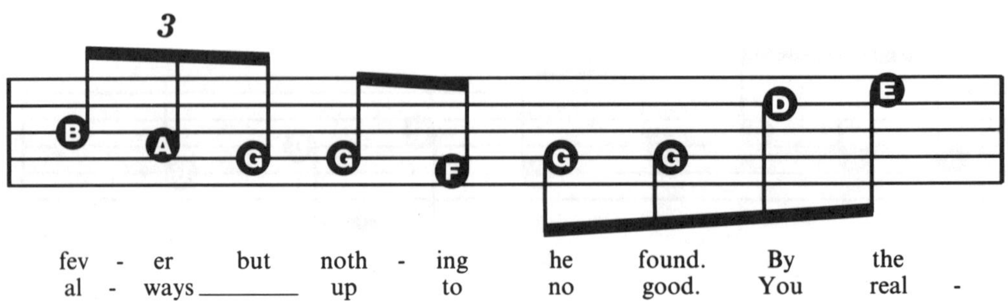
3
fev - er but noth - ing he found. By the
al - ways up to no good. You real -

time this hit the street, they
ly can't make him hate her, so your

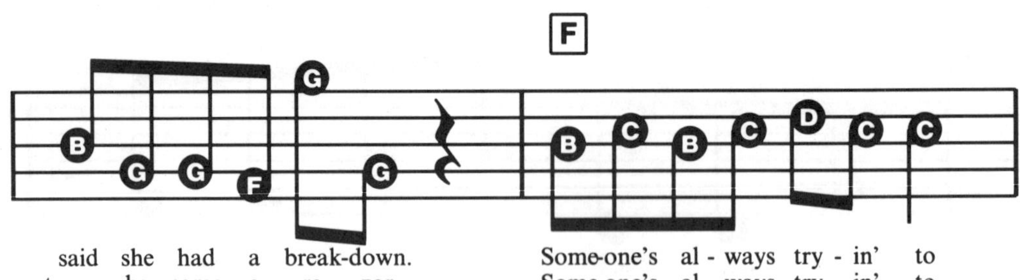
F
said she had a break-down. Some-one's al - ways try - in' to
tongue be - came a ra - zor. Some-one's al - ways try - in' to

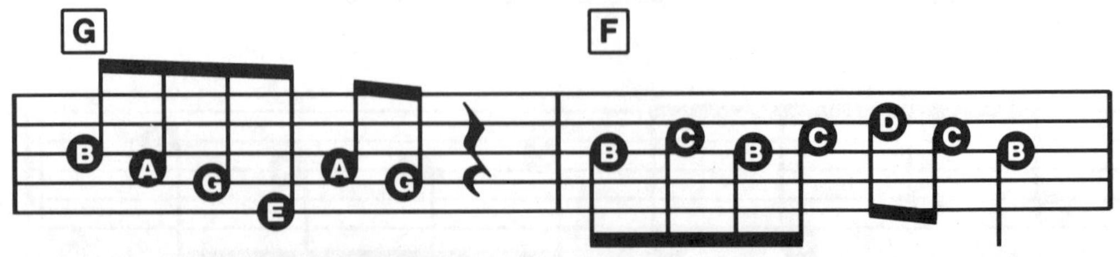
G
F
start my ba - by cry - in'. Talk - in', squeal-in', ly - in, sayin'
keep my ba - by cry - in'. Treacher-ous cun - nin' declin - in' You

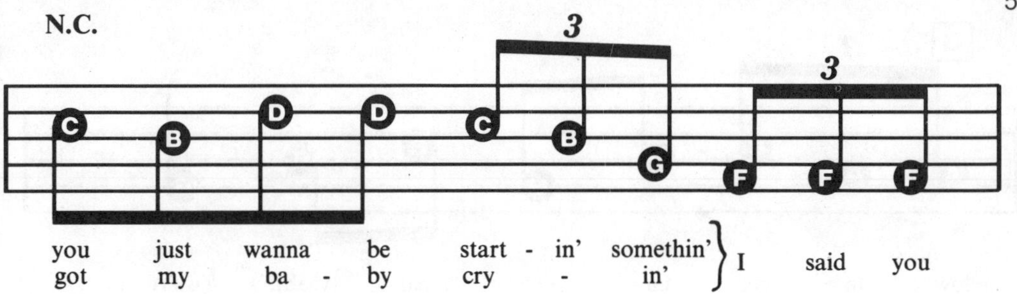
N.C.
3
C B D D C B G F F F
you just wanna be start - in' somethin'
got my ba - by cry - in'
I said you

Chorus

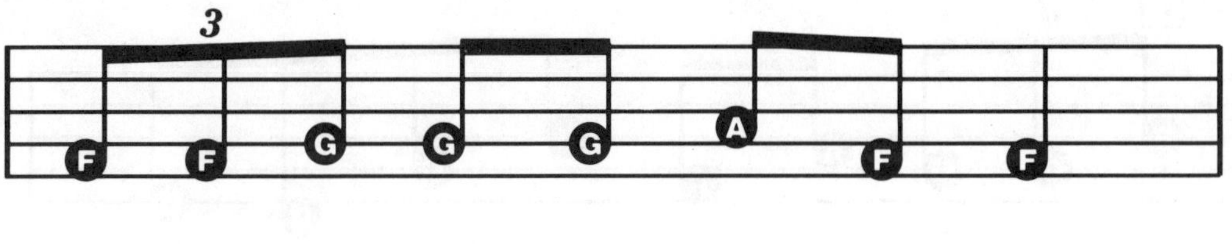
3
F F G G G A F F
wan - na be start - in' some - thin', you

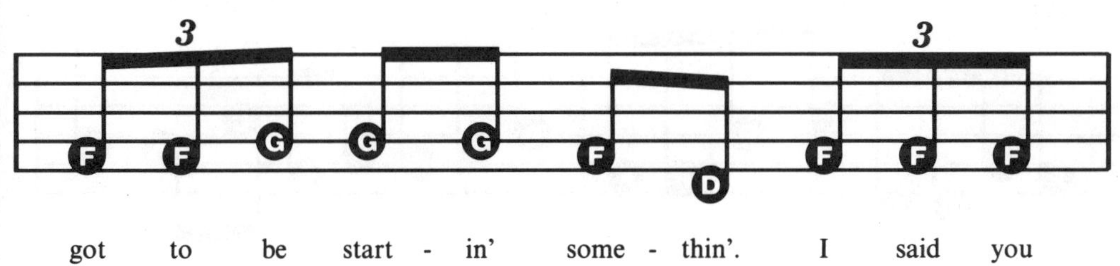
3
F F G G G F D F F F
got to be start - in' some - thin'. I said you

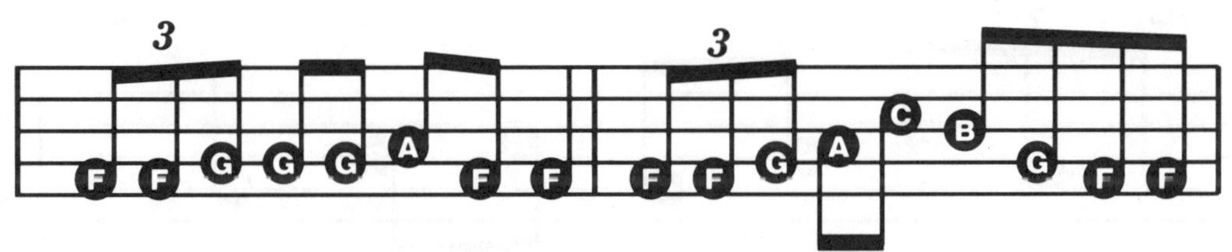
3
F F G G G A F F F F G A C B G F F
wan - na be start - in' some-thin', you got to be start - in' some-thin'. It's too

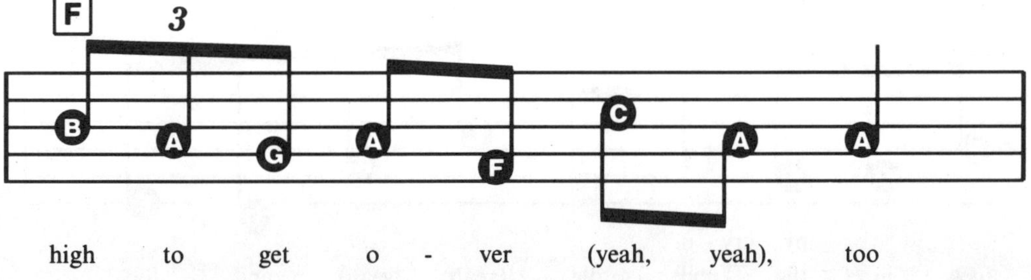
F
3
B A G A F C A A
high to get o - ver (yeah, yeah), too

G
3
A A C B G C B G
low to get un - der (yeah, yeah). You're
F
3
B G G A F B G D E
stuck in the mid - dle (yeah, yeah), and the
G
F G D D C B F F
pain is thun-der (yeah, yeah). It's too
F
3
B A G A F C A A
high to get o - ver (yeah, yeah), too
G
3
A A C B G C B G
low to get un - der (yeah, yeah). You're
F
3
B G G A F C A D E
stuck in the mid - dle (yeah, yeah), and the

1.
G
pain is thun - der (yeah, yeah). 2. You
2,3.
G
F
pain is thun - der (yeah, yeah). You're a veg' - ta - ble, you're a
G
F
veg' - ta - ble. Still they hate you. You're a
G
F
veg' - ta - ble. You're a buf - fet, you're a
G
F
veg' - ta - ble. They eat off of you. You're a

61

N.C.
3
F D D
F G G D F G
veg' - ta - ble.

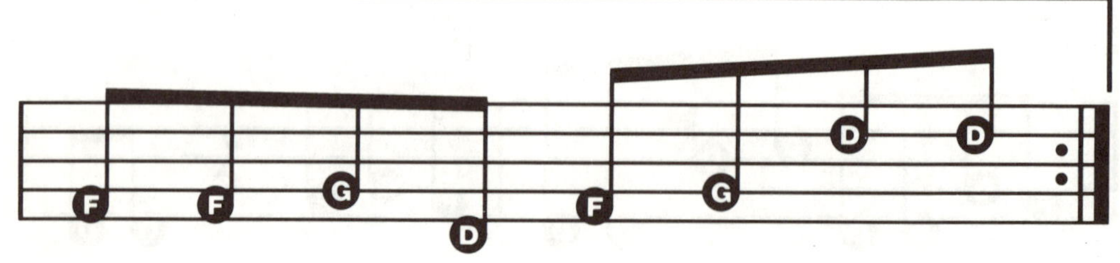
F F G D F G D D
3. Bil - ie
4. If you

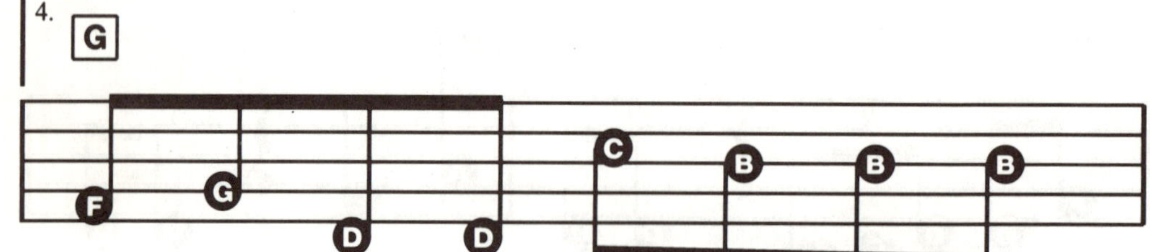
4.
G
F G D D C B B B
pain is thun - der (yeah, yeah). Lift your

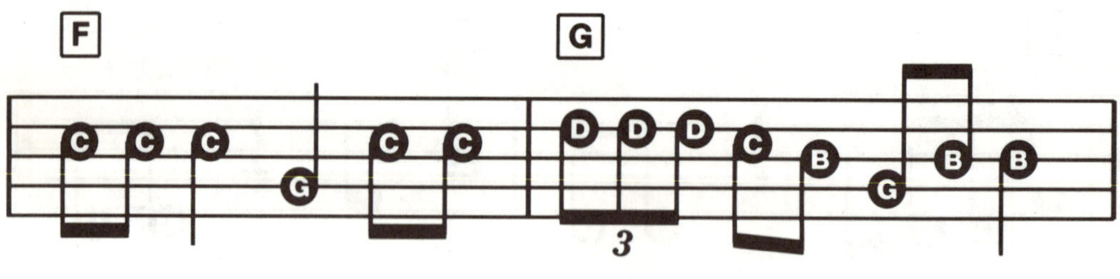
F
G
C C C G C C D D D C B G B B
3
head up high and scream out to the world, "I know I

F
G
C C C G C C D D D B B B
am some-one!" and let the truth un - furl. No - one can

Flute + Piccola

My own Tune (The Skating Swan)

by D. Alker

repeat again

Then

Then play the first again for the ending

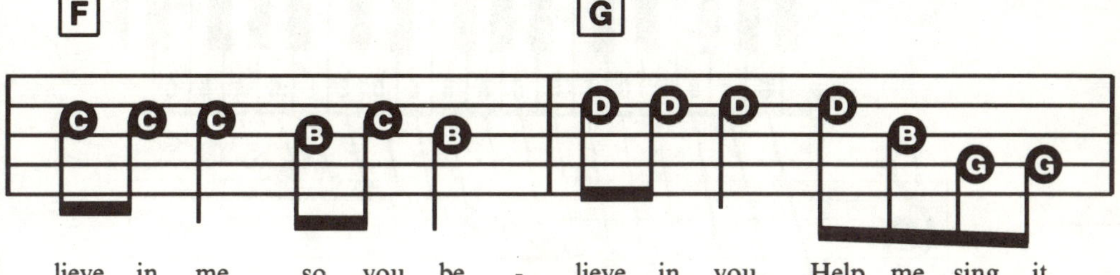

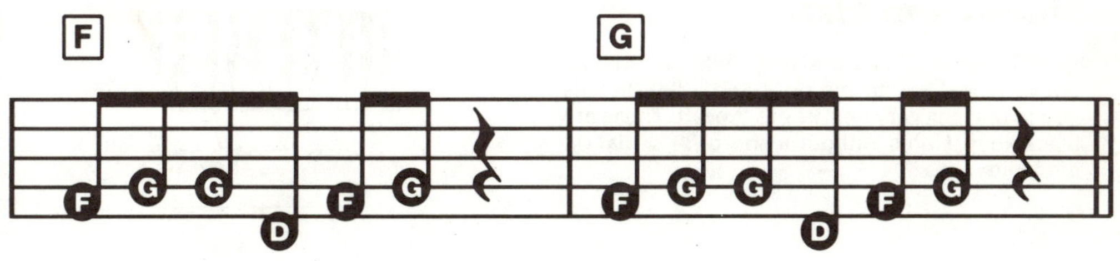

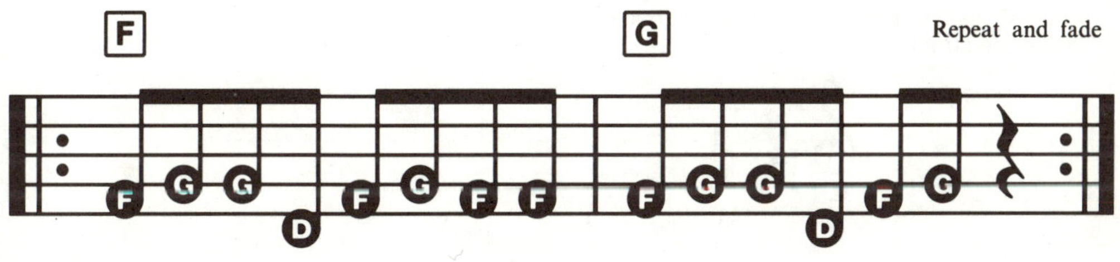

Additional Lyrics

3. Billie Jean is always talkin'
When nobody else is talkin',
Tellin' lies and rubbin' shoulders,
So they call her mouth a motor.
Someone's always tryin'
To start my baby cryin'
Talkin, squealin', spyin', sayin' you
just wanna be startin' somethin'
I said you
(To Chorus)

4. If you can't feed your baby
Then don't have a baby.
And don't think maybe,
If you can't feed your baby.
You'll be always tryin'
To stop that child from cryin'.
Nustlin', stealin', lyin'.
Now baby's slowly dyin'.
I said you
(To Chorus)

HE ABC's OF

The Melody (Right Hand)

The melody appears as large lettered notes. The letter name corresponds to a key on your keyboard.

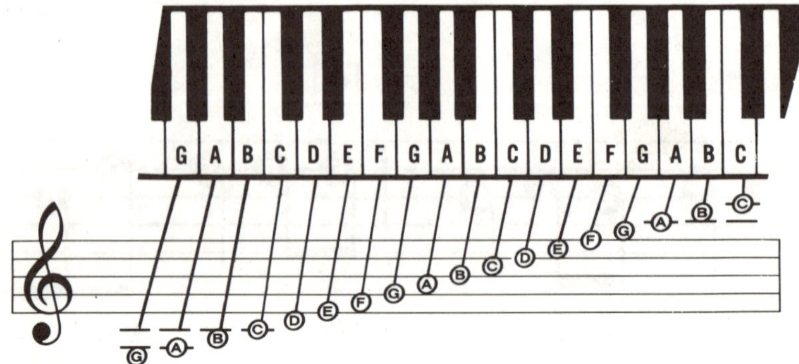

Sharps and Flats

In LETTER MUSIC a **sharp** (♯) tells you to play the very next key to the right and a **flat** (♭) tells you to play the very next key to the left. These are black keys. Notes without a **sharp** (♯) or **flat** (♭) are white keys.

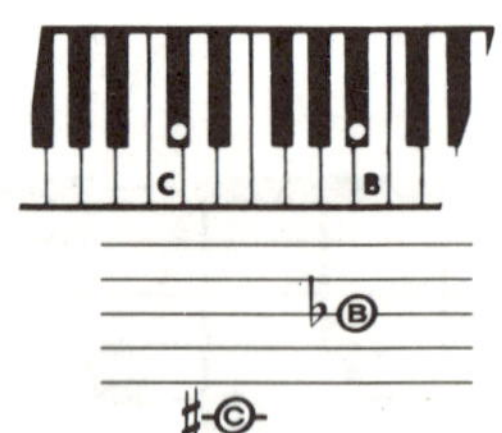

Ties

A **tie** is a curved line connecting notes on the same line or in the same space. It indicates the first note is struck and then held for the total time value of the tied notes. Only notes with a letter inside are struck.

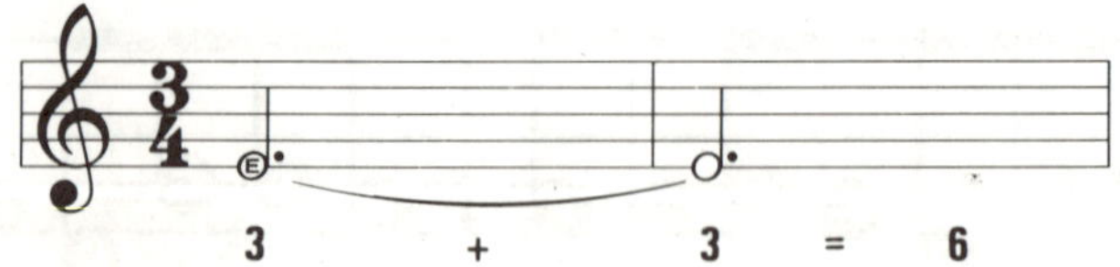

The Accompaniment (Left Hand)

The accompaniment consists of chords. All the major and minor chords you need to play appear inside a box. Optional seventh (7) chords appear outside the box.

C G7 Cm Gm7

N.C. tells you "No Chord" is played — just the right-hand melody.

Generally, there are three ways to play chords: One finger, traditional, and three-note Easy-Play chords. Your owner's guide can help you decide which methods your keyboard is capable of. Be sure to try them all.